Financial Accounting

Financial Accounting

B.G. Satyaprasad
Professor and Director
GT Institute of Management Studies and Research
Bangalore

Vedananda Murthy
Professor of Commerce
SLN College
Bangalore

K. Janardhanam
Director
Canara Bank School of Management Studies
Bangalore University
Bangalore

C.S. Anantaram
Head
Mathematics Academy
Tumkur

TECHSAR™
NEW DELHI

Published and Printed by

TechSar Pvt. Ltd.
4435-36/7, Ansari Road, Daryaganj
New Delhi–110 002 (India)
E-mail: tech_info@techsarworld.com
Website: www.techsarworld.com

ISBN: 978-93-82332-07-7

Reprint 2025

Foreword

The subject Financial Accounting provides management with data needed to determine whether a business is at loss or profit, how much debtors owe, how much a business owes others, and other financial information. Accounting measures business transactions and as such can help steer managers in the right direction with solid information, not gut feelings. Basically, accounting is a tool for management to employ to help make sound business decisions on a timely manner. For instance, if by using accounting information, managers notice that the trend is for sales to decrease, then they can take measures to stop this trend. May be they need to change price or decrease expenses to handle the downtrend. The key is that accounting gave them the clue that something may not be going according to plan, playing an important role in business management.

Till the year 1992, India practised conservative economic policies and later adopted liberalization, privatization and globalization policies. As a result of this, India witnessed unprecedented economic growth. Huge employment opportunities were created in IT, construction, infrastructure, aviation, business process management and so on. This created the necessity to equip our youth with new set of knowledge and skills.

In the era of ever changing business environment the student must keep his knowledge updated on a continuous basis. From this academic year onwards Bangalore University has updated its B.Com and BBM syllabus which matches the contemporary business environment.

Financial Accounting is as per the new syllabus. The book includes various aspects of accounting including accounting principles, accounting concepts, accounting conventions, and so on.

The subject of Financial Accounting is vast and exhaustive. Authors of this book have attempted to give brief and specific information as per the requirements of the university students. Appropriate examples have been used to drive the message to the student.

It is a question of pride and delight for me because one of the authors is the Head of G.T. Group of Institutions, Bangalore. All the authors of this book have done excellent work to bring out this book and I hope the students will make the best use of this book.

S. T. Anand
Chairman
G.T. Group of Institutions
G.T. Industrial Enterprises
G.T. Cinemas Pvt Ltd
G.T. Mall and Multiplex

Preface

"The system of book-keeping by double entry is, perhaps, the most beautiful one in the wide domain of literature or science. Were it less common, it would be the admiration of the learned world."

Edwin T. Freedley (1827–1904), US manufacturer
Source: *A Practical Treatise on Business* (1853)

Accounting is literally the lifeblood of any business, without knowing where a company stands financially, a manager, a CEO, or the owner cannot operate business to its fullest potential. The financial statements used in accounting are like a photograph of the company's financial standing at any given period.

Accounting provides management with data needed to determine whether a business is at loss or profit, how much debtors owe, how much a business owes others, and other important financial information for decision making. Accounting measures business transactions and as such can help managers to steer in the right direction with information and not based on gut feelings. Basically, accounting is a tool for management to make sound business decisions. Accounting gives the decision makers a wider view of the situation playing an important role in business management.

While writing this book, we have balanced the theoretical concepts and practical illustrations which are relevant for students. We have tried to be simple and to the point, so that it is easy to grasp the concepts. We have summarized the content at the end of each chapter, which we are hopeful will be handy to the teachers as well as the learners.

We welcome any suggestions from the teachers and students to improve this book. You can mail your valuable feedback to: info.gteducation@gmail.com.

Authors

Contents

Authors

B.G. Satyaprasad M.Com, MBA, Ph.D

B.G. Satyaprasad, 'finance guru' as his students fondly call him, is an outstanding academician of repute who is also decorated with 'Best Teacher' award (2003) by the Govt. of Karnataka for the exceptional services rendered by him in the field of commerce and management education. A prolific writer who has authored over twenty-five books in the area of commerce and management. He has also guided several M.Phil and Ph.D scholars. He is guiding several educational institutions in India to achieve excellence in the quality of education. He is a consultant for accreditation and quality certifications such as NAAC, NBA, and ISO etc. He is an expert in establishing institutions for higher education. He is also known as an authority on distance learning programme. He has designed and established distance education programmes for several universities. He has served many committees of UGC and other leading universities in enhancing the quality of higher education. Currently he is serving as Director at GT Group of Institutions, Bangalore.

Vedananda Murthy M.Com, EMBA, Ph.D

One of the seniormost teachers in the area of commerce having over 3 decades of experience in academics. Currently serving as a Professor of Commerce in SLN First Grade College, Bangalore.

He has participated, presented research papers in many state & national level conferences.

He has been awarded a Doctorate by Bangalore University in Finance for his research work on 'Asset Liability Management of Commercial Banks'.

K. Janardhanam

A researcher and a seasoned academician having more than twenty-five years of experience in teaching and research in commerce and management area. Currently he is serving as a Director, Canara Bank School of Management Studies at Bangalore University. He has served the university in various capacities such as academic council, senate and syndicate member. His area of specialization is Finance and Accounting. He has guided several MPhil and PhD scholars.

C.S. Anantaram

A veteran mathematician, Head, Mathematics Academy at Tumkur, has trained thousands of students in mathematics. He has authored several books on the area of Business Mathematics, Vedic Mathematics and Quantitative Techniques. He has contributed as subject expert in designing the curriculum and content of the study material for High School level in Karnataka State. He has presented, chaired several state, national and international conferences.

He has conducted several workshops and guided, trained and educated teachers to teach mathematics and quantitative techniques.

1

Introduction to Financial Accounting

1.1 INTRODUCTION

Every businessman irrespective of nature and size of his business wants to know whether his business is running under profit or not, and whether his financial position is sound or otherwise. In order to ensure profitability or otherwise of his business, an income statement or profit and loss account is prepared. Similarly, to ensure his financial status at a particular moment of time, a balance sheet is prepared. Moreover, this accounting information is required to evaluate the operational efficiency or otherwsie of the business and also solvency of the business. This information can be provided only when business transactions are recorded, classified and summarised properly.

In order to achieve the above goals, the preliminary work involved in the entire process accounting starts with recording bsuiness transactions according to a well derived system, i.e., bookkeeping (on elementary stage) and accounting (latter stage) is the name given to such a system.

Meaning and Definition of Bookkeeping

Bookkeeping, the aspect of recording transactions, i.e., the pratical aspect, is an art of recording transactions in a set of financial books so that a permanent record is maintained in the business. The elementary part of work in the whole process of accounting is performed by a bookkeeper who is mainly concerned with:

1. journalising
2. posting to ledger
3. totalling of different accounts in the ledger
4. balancing of accounts

1.2 DEFINITION OF BOOKKEEPING

In the words of R.N. Carter, "Bookkeeping is the science and art of correctly recording in the books of accounts all those tansactions that result in the transfer of money or money's worth."

1.3 MEANING AND DEFINITION OF ACCOUNTING

The work of an accountant begins where bookkeeping ends. It means that an acountant comes into picture only when the bookkeeper has done his job. An accountant has to go behind the work of a bookkeeper and satisfy himself that the transactions have been properly recorded, posted into concerned books of account. His duty lies in making the trial balance agree and prepare profit and loss account and balance sheet after making necessary adjustments and rectification of errors.

In short it can be stated that he has to prepare the summary of accounts in the form of trial balance and make an analysis after prepaing profit and loss account and balance sheet. An accountant is expected to be an expert in the accounting procedures as he has to examine analytically the final accounts.

According to *The American Institute of Chartered Public Accountants*, accounting "is an art of recording, classifiying and summarising, in a significant manner and in terms of money, transactions and events which are, in part at least of a financial character and interpreting results thereof ".

Therefore, it is clear from the above definition that accounting is the recording, classifying and summarising of business transactions and interpreting the results thereof.

1.4 DIFFERENCE BETWEEN BOOKKEEPING AND ACCOUNTING

Points difference	Book-keeping	Accounting
1. Meaning	– is an art of recording monetary transactions in	– is concerned with the deisign of the systems of records, classification and

(Contd.)

(Contd.)

	a set of books.	summarising financial data into reports and communicating the results thereof.
2. Nature	– routine and clerical	– technical and complicated
3. Scope	– of book-keeping is narrow or original records of usiness transactions	– of accounting is wider than bookkeeping and it includes bookkeeping also.
4. Object	– aims at creating primary	– aims at checking the arithmetical accuracy of the transactions recorded so as to present reliable results.
5. Conclusion	– does not provide financial statement viz., profit and loss account and balance sheet.	– is mainly concerned with the preparation of finanical statements-profit and loss account and balance sheet and their analysis and interpretation.

1.5 OBJECTIVES OF ACCOUNTING

The following are the objectives of accounting:

1. To maintain the accurate and permanent record of business transactions
2. To ascertain the profit or loss of the business for an accounting period
3. To assess the financial status of the business, i.e., strength or weakness of financial position of the business
4. To know what amount is owed by the business to the outsiders and what amount is due from outsiders to the business
5. To know progress or otherwise of the business from year to year
6. To prevent the occurrence of erro rs and frauds
7. To compute tax liability due to the government
8. To have valuable information for future planning
9. To guide or determine dividend action
10. To provide important information for granting credit to the business

Role or Functions of Accounting

The functions of an accounting may be grouped as:

(a) Primary functions

(b) Subsidiary functions

(a) Primary Functions

The primary functions of accounting are:

1. Creation of systematic record: Accounting supplements human memory by creating permanent record of business tansactions in an analytical and appropriate manner. This record can be refered to, any number of times in future.

2. Protection to properties of business: By maintaining proper record of various properties belonging to the business, an accountant enables the management to exercise proper control over the use of properties of the business (i.e., preventing wrong use of the property).

3. Communication of financial results: Accounting communicates the financial results such as profilt or loss and the finanial position of business to the various parties interested in financial statements; like shareholders, debenture holders, creditors, investors, employees, taxation authorities and other government agencies. Hence, accounting is regarded as the language of business.

4. Legal requirements: Various acts of Parliament (statues) under which business organisations are established (such as Indian Companies Act 1956, the Banking Regulation Act, 1949 etc.) are required to comply with statue. The provisions of various laws i.e., income-tax act, sales tax act, SEBI, etc., require the business concern to maintain necessary records and submit financial reports. Therefore, accounting meets legal requirements.

(b) Subsidiary Functions

The following are the subsidiary functions of accounting:

1. Legal evidence: The books of accounts can be produced as evidence in support of case laws filed against the business concern and also before the taxation authorities.

2. Regulation of business activities: Accounting reports enable the management to evaluate and control the peformance of the business. The accounting records and techniques are very much useful in regulating the business activities.

3. Trend analysis: The financial data of several years can be used to facilitate comparison of sales, costs, and operating profits of the business enterprise through the trend percentages. Such comparison helps the management to measure the trend—upward or downward and reasons for the same.

4. Computation of income tax: The financial statements or reports enable the taxation authorities to compute easily tax to be imposed on a business enterprise. This relieves the business people from unnecessary harassment by the taxation authorities.

5. Easy borrowing: Banks and other financial institutions base their decisions regarding the sanction of loan, amount of loan, repayment period, etc., on the accounting information furnished by the business concerns from time to time.

6. Decision-making: Accounting provides relevant information to the parties interested in it such as shareholders, management, financial institutions, investors, etc., and enable them to take their own decisions.

1.7 USERS OF ACCOUNTING INFORMATION

Accounting provides useful information regarding the business enterprise to the parties who are interested in operational results as well as the financial position of the business. Such parties may be share holders, management, creditors, investors, government employees, researchers and general public.

1. Shareholders (owners): The owners of the business provide funds or capital needed for the business purpose. They are interested in two things, namely, (i) safety of their investment and (ii) regular return on their investment. So, they possess curiosity in knowing whether the business is being conducted on sound lines or not. Comparing accounts of several years helps them in getting correct information.

2. Management: The accounts are the basis on which the management can study the merits and drawbacks of their business activities. Moreso, the management of the business is greatly interested in knowing the position of the business—profitability position and financial position.

Thus, the management is interested in accounting information to find whether the business carried on is profitable or not. The financial statements are, *the eyes and ears of management and facilitate in drawing the future course of action, further expansion, etc.*

3. Creditors: Creditors are those to whom the business owes money—suppliers bankers and other lenders of money. It is usual that these parties are interested to know financial soundness before granting credit. The progress and prosperity of the firm, to which credits are extended are largely wanted by creditors from the point of view of security and prompt repayment

4. Employees: Hike in salaries, payment of bonus and demand for other fringe benefits depend up on amount of profit earned by the firm. The more important point is that the employees expect regular income for their bread and butter. The demand for rise in salaries/wages, bonus, better working conditions, etc., depend upon the profitability of the firm, and therefore, they are very much interested in accounting information.

5. Investors: The prospective investor who wants to invest his hard earned money in a firm depends much upon the progress and prosperity of the firm before investing his money. Accounting reports enable the investor to study the safety or otherwise of their investment.

6. Government: The state and central governments are interested in the financial statements to know the earnings of an enterprise for the purpose of taxation and other duties to be imposed.

7. Consumers: Consumers are interested in getting the goods at reduced prices. Therefore, they with to know the establishment of proper accounting control which in turn will reduce cost of production and ultimately the prices to be paid by them.

8. Stock exchange: The financial statements are the blueprints of financial affairs of a business concern. These statements enable the stock exchange to protect interest of investors or to watch as watchdog of corporate investors.

9. Research scholars: Researchers are also interested in interpretation of accounting information.

10. Professional societies: Professional societies like Chamber of Commerce, Indian Accounting Association, employees association, banks, financial institutions, etc., are deeply interested in such financial statements of an enterprise.

1.8 LIMITATIONS OF ACCOUNTING

Financial accounting suffers from the following limitations which have been responsible for the emergence of cost accounting and management accounting.

1. Historical in nature: Financial statements are based on historical cost, and as such the impact of price level changes are ignored. For example, building purchased for Rs. 1,00,000 continues to appear at Rs. 1,00,000 only (even after a gap of several years) or not at market price.

2. Interim reports: Profits disclosed by profit and loss account and financial position exhibited by the balance sheet cannot be exact, they are essentially interim reports, Exact position can be known only when the business is liquidated, i.e., is closed down its shutters.

3. Provides only quantitative information: Information disclosed by financial accounting is incomplete because it provides only quantitative information (i.e., information about monetary transactions). Non-monetary transactions (qualitative factors) such as reputation of the business with public, efficiency and loyalty of employees, integrity of the management, etc., which are equally important for business success do not find place in financial accounting.

4. Unreliable information: Information provided by financial accounting is not realistic The reason being, the accounting statements are prepared by following certain conventions and concepts, e.g., *on account of "convention of conservatism"* the income statement may not show true income of the business since the probable losses are considered while probable incomes are ignored. Similarly, the fixed assets are shown at cost less depreciation on the basis of '*going concern concept*'. But the values placed on fixed assets may not be the same which may be realised on their sale.

5. Role of personal judgement: Personal judgement of an accountant who is responsible for the preparation of accounts limits the utility of financial statements. For instance, provision for depreciation, valuation of stock on hand, bad debts provision etc., depend upon the personal judgement of an accountant.

6. Provides information of the business as a whole: Financial accounting provides information regarding results of an enterprise as a whole. But it does not provide detailed cost information for different departments, processes, products, jobs in production division. The management may need information about different products, sales territories, etc., which are not available in financial accounting.

7. Control of costs is not possible: It difficult to know the behaviour of costs in financial accounting, as expenses are calculated after incurring theym and not before incurring them. As such control of cost which is the most important objective of all business enterprises, cannot be achieved with the aid of financial accounts alone.

8. Does not provide information to analyse losses: Financial accounting does not provide information to analyse the losses due to various factors such as idle plant, and equipment, seasonal fluctuations in the volume of business, etc. It does not help the management in taking important decisions about the expansion of business, dropping a product line innovation a new product, alternative methods of production, improvement of existing products, etc. Managerial decision about these business matters are vital for survival and growth of the business enterprise.

1.9 ACCOUNTING PRINCIPLES, CONCEPTS AND CONVENTIONS

Knowledge of basic terms used in 'Accounting' is a must for any one if he or she were to understand 'Accounting terminology'. The following are the basic terms used in 'Accounting terminology'. The following are the basic terms used in 'Accounting':

1. Transactions: is a business dealing whih involvcs transfer of money or money's work from one person to another.

Essential features of transactions:

1. There must be two parties.
2. There must be transfer goods or anything with money

3. Effet of transaction should be expressed in monetary terms.

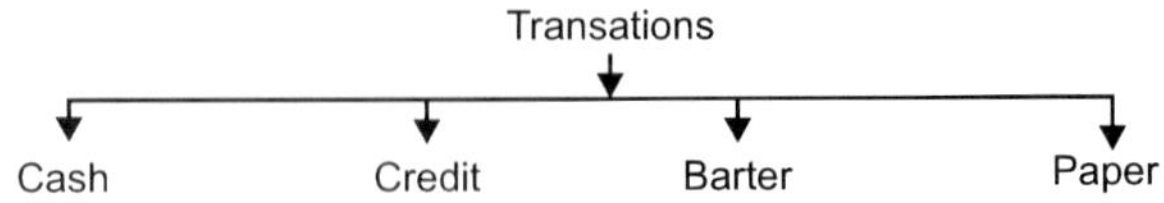

(a) Cash Cransactions: is a business dealing which involves immediate cash payment. It is also called as 'complete transaction' becuase there remains no relationship between buyer and seller.

e.g. purchase of goods for cash ₹ 10,000.

(b) Credit Transactions: is a bsuiness dealing, where payment of cash is postphoned or deferred to a future date. This transaction is also called as incomplete transaction because there remains the relationship between the buyer and seller till the settlement (i.e. payment of cash).

e.g. sold goods to Rama on Credit ₹ 5,000.

(c) Barter Transaction: This tranaction do not involve money as a medium of exchange. Under this transaction goods are exchanged for goods or services areexchanged for services. in other words, goods or services to be exchanged are expressed in terms of money. these transactions were present before introducing money as medium of exchange i.e., Barter economy.

e.g. Exchange of machinery for motor car.

(d) Paper transaction: is one which do not involve any exchange of money or money's worth between the parties. More so, the presence of parties such as receiver and giver is not necessary.

e.g. Depreiating provided on fixed assets loss of goods due to fire accident etc.

2. Entity: means identity or identifications of existence of a business unit. A firm or a business enterprise has a peperate entity distinct firm owners of the business.

3. Firm/Enterprise/Concern: Any organisaton an Entity which deals with business i.e., an economic activity is called as firm/enterprise/concern'. e.g., sole trading concern, partnership firm, joint stock company etc.

4. Goods: Means the commodities on whih the traders deals.

e.g., Textile merchant clothes or textile in which deals are goods furniture merchant - furniture in which he deals is goods.

5. Capital: Money or money's worth introduced by the properietor or owner int his business.

Here, money' worth means stock of goods, furniture, machinery or any other asset introduced into the business.

Excess of Assets over liabilities of a business is also called capital.

6. Propretor of Business: A proprietor is an individual or a person who contributes money (capital) or money's worth-assets to the business. He is also called as owner of the business.

7. Drawings: Means cash or goods withdrawn by the owner of the business from his business for his personaluse of domestic purpose.

8. Assets: Means the resources or properties owned and possessed by the business enterprise. For carrying on usiness. In otherwords resources through which income is generated by a business enterprise, or any thing acquired by business enterprise for permanent use in the business.

Assets are basically classified into two categories, namely, (a) Tangible assets and (b) Intangible assets.

(a) Tangible assets: are those assets which can be seen, touched or used. They are the properties physically existing with business enterprise. Examples—land, building, plant, machinery, motor vehicles, furniture, fixtures, fittings, cash in hand, cash at bank, stock of goods, amount due from customers (debtors), bills receivable etc.

(b) Intangible assets: are those assets which are invisible or which cannot be seen or touched or felt, but are equally important to the business like any tangible asset. Examples—goodwill, trad marks, copy rights, patent rights etc.

The assets of a business concern are further classified as:

(a) Fixed assets
(b) Current assets
(c) liquid or quick assets
(d) Wasting assets
(e) Ficitious assets and
(f) Contingent assets.

(a) Fixed assets: are those assets which are acquired for permanent and continuous use in the business. They are the assets which are acquired for generating income. they are neither meant for resale in the ordinary course of business nor consumed totally or partially in the business. e.g. land, building, plant, machinery, furniture etc.

(b) Curretn or floating or circulating assets: These are the assets which cannot be put to constant use. These assets are meant for resale. These are meant for conversion into cash. e.g. bookdebts, stock of goods, bills recievable etc.

(c) Liquid or quick assets: are the assets which can be converted into cash within a short span of time without much loss e.g. csh, bank balance, bills recivable. They consist all current assets except stock.

(d) Wasting assets: are those assets which exhaust by working and hence, the process involves depletion of capital. In otherwords, decrease in value of such asset is a result of operating of extracting a part of it or gradual exhaustion.

(e) Fictitious assets: are differnt by their nature itself. They are the assets which are not physically visible. Though the money is spent thereon, they fetch nothing i.e., they are unrealisable.
Example: Preliminary exprenses, dicount on issue of shares and debentures, undercoliters commission on issue of shares, issue expenses of shares etc. These assets are also known as nominal assets or deferred revenue expenditure.

(f) Contingent Assets: are not the true assets of the business. They may or may not become the true assets. Becoming true asset or otherwise depends upon the event to happen. They are not shown infinancial statement e.g. claim for tax refund.

9. Liability: is the word derived from French word 'lier' which means 'to bind'. Therefore, liability is the amount owed by a businessman to outsiders—suppliers, financial institutions etc.

Examples: Creditors, Bills payable, Bank overdebt etc.

A liability is of 5 categories; namely;

(a) Trade liability
(b) Non-trade liability
(c) Long-term liability
(d) Short-term or current liability
(e) Contingent liability

(a) Trade liability: is the liability which arises whey the goods are purchased on credit.
Example: If textile merchant purchases textiles on credit, the liability arising therefrom is a trade liability.

(b) Non-Trade liability: is the liability which arises when something other than the goods are purchased on credit.
Example: Shen textile merchant purchases furniture on credit, the liability arising there from is a non-trade liability.

(c) Long-term liability: is a liability which is repayable after the expiry of relatively long period.
Examples: Mortgage loom, long-term looms borrowed, Debentures resaved by a company etc.

(d) Short-term liability: is liability which should be repaid within a short span of time i.e., within 12 months, the maximum.
Examples: Creditors, Bills Payable, Bank overdraft, etc.

(e) Contingent liabilities: are not the ture liabilities of the business they may or may not become be liabilities of the business. their becoming liability or otherwise depends up on the event to happen
Example: Guarantee given for loans borrowed by third parties.

10. Equity: means claims against the assets of the firm. Equity is of 2 types namely: (a) Owners' equity and (b) outsiders equity.

(a) Owners' Equity: shre of owners in the propertres of on enterprise.
(b) Outsiders' equity: share of outsiders' in the prperties of an enterprise.

11. Debtors: Debtors is a person who owes money to the business.

12. Creditors: is a person to whom the business owes money.

13. Debt: Amount due from a customer of the business called debtor.

14. Purchases: Purchase of goods for the business are called purchases. goods, here, means the commodities in which the trader deals.

15. Sales: is the amount realised by sale of goods exclusively. However, sale of anything other than goods, cannot be treated as sales.

16. Purchase Returns: when the purchaser of goods returns defective or damanged goods to the suppose it is called as purchase returns.

17. Sales Returns: the seller receives damaged or defective goods returned by his customers after affecting a sale is called 'sales returns',

18. Investments: when a business may purchases shares and securities of public ltd companies or government boyds to avoid keeping funds idle on the business is lifixed as 'Investments'.

19. Expense: An expanse means money spent for enjoying some benefit.
Example: paid ₹ 25 to buy a bus ticket travel 5 kilometers. hence ₹ 25 to is money spent, and 5 kilometers travel benefit.

20. Stock of goods: goods remained unsale with the business at the end of accounting year are called stock of goods.

21. Profits: is Excess of income of revenue over expenditure.

22. Loss: is excess of expenditure over income or revenue.

23. Depreciation: means the decrease in the value of a fixed asset due to wear and tear or constant use. This is treated as loss and charged to profit and loss account.

24. Account: An account is the summarised record of transaction. 'A/c' is the abbreviation used for denoting the name of the a/c. Account is prepared in 'T' from left hand side of an account is called debit side expressed on left corner of an account as 'on' and right hand side of an account is called crdit side expressed on right corner of an account as "Cr."

25. Head of Account: Name of the account to be written as the top and cntre of an account i.e. 'T' is called of an account'.

26. Debit: means 'to charge an account'. Inother words, making entry on left hand side of an account.

27. Credit: means 'to entitle an account'. In otherwords making entry on right hand side of an account.

28. Trial Balance: It is a statement of ledger balances prepared at end of every accounting year to check the arithematical accuracy of accounts.

29. Voucher: is a documntary evidence in support of the transactions recorded in book of prime entry.

30. Entry: means second of transactions is the journal.

31. Journal: All the transactions of the business are recorded first is the book meant for the purpose is called journal. Journal is also called as a 'day book' or a book of 'prime entry' or 'original entry' or 'First entry'.

32. Ledger: It is book meant for maining various accounts of the business enterprise. Ledger is also called as a book of 'final entry' or 'last entry'.

33. Posting: The out of recording entry from journal in the ledger is called 'posting' in otherwords, of means transfer of an entry from journal to ledger.

34. Net worth: Excess of business assets over business liabilities as on a particular (ie., end of an accounting year) is called networth.

35. Solvent: Solvent is one who capable of discharging all his business liabilities.

36. Insolvent: is one who usable to discharge his business liabilities. In other words, insolvent is a person whose liabilities are more than his assets.

37. Folio: means page number of a journal or ledger where a particular entry is made or particular account is prepared.

38. Jounalising: The process of recording the transaction in the book of journal is called 'jounalising'.

Accounting Principles—Meaning and Definition

Principle means the fundamental truth implying uniformity of acceptance everywhere. It cannotes guiding influence, or an accepted rule of action or conduct. So, accounting principles are broad guidelines or rules of action to be adopted by accountants for the preparation of accounts and for the presentation of financial statements.

GAAPS: Accounting principles are a set of rules and guidelines which are widely accepted by accounting practitioners (chartered accountants) at a given time. Therefore, they are called "*Generally Accepted Accounting Principles—GAAPS*".

According to AICPA (US): A principle means "a general law or rule adopted or professed as a guide to action, a settled ground or basis of conduct or practice."

Accounting principle or accounting standard should always satisfy the following three rules, namely:

1. usefulness or relevance
2. objectivity
3. feasibility

1. Usefulness or relevance: The 'standard' must cater to the carefulness of accounting statements. In other words, the statements must be meaningful to the users of the same.

2. Objectivity: The accounting standards should have objectivity, i.e., they should be supported and supplemented by basic facts or data and not by whims of individuals who prepare accounts or statements.

3. Feasibility: The accounting standards must be practicable or feasible to attain. For example, inventory should be valued at cost price or market price whichever is less. This is determined on the basis of feasibility.

1.11 CHARACTERISTICS OF ACCOUNTING PRINCIPLES

1. Accounting principles are made and developed by man. (i.e., an accountant) and as such, they do not have authoritativeness, as universal principles like other natural sciences i.e., physics, chemistry, mathematics, etc.
2. Accounting principles are developed for common usage to ensure uniformity and understandability and to facilitate comparison.
3. The principles are not specifically made or enhanced by any authority.
4. The principles are in the process of evolution.
5. They are not rigid.
6. The principles should be generally acceptable and for the purpose, these three rules—usefulness, objectivity and feasibility must have to be fulfilled.

1.12 CLASSIFICATION OF ACCOUNTING PRINCIPLES

The accounting principles can be classified into two categories, namely:

(a) Accounting concepts
(b) Accounting conventions

(a) Accounting Concepts

The term 'concept includes those basic assumptions (or postulates or notions or mental ideas about something) and conditions upon which the science of accounting is based.

Following are the important accounting concepts:

1. Business entity concept
2. Going concern concept
3. Money measurement concept
4. Cost concept
5. Accounting period concept
6. Dual aspect concept
7. Matching concept
8. Realisation concept
9. Verifiable or objective evidence concept
10. Acrual concept.

1. Business entity concept: Under this concept, it is assumed that business unit is distinct and completely separate from its owners who invest money or any other assets in the business. In this case, proprietor of the business is considered an outsider. It is with this reason, his investment in the business is called capital—liability. Similarly, his drawings (withdrawals for personal use from the business) will be charged to him. For example, if he has invested Rs. 20,000—treated as capital, his drawings Rs. 5,000 is treated as charge. Hence, net amount payable by business to the proprietor is shown as Rs. 15,000 only.

The concept of separate entity is applicable to all forms of business organisation. Sole trader of sole trading concern, or partner of a partnership firm are not considered separate entities in the eyes of law, but for the accounting pruposes they will be considered separate entities. The joint stock company has a separate entity in the eyes of law because on 'company is an artificial person created by law'.

2. Going concern concept: This concept assumes that the business entity as a continuity of life or future of business enterprise is extended indefinitely and not to liquidate the affairs. On account of this concept, an accountant does not take into account forced sale of value of assets, rather the fixed assets are shown at cost less depriciation.

According to this concept, assets are required for permanent and continuous use in the business and therefore, market value or realisable value of assets is not considered for the purpose of valuation of assets.

Further, all outstanding expenses and incomes, prepaid expenses and prereceived incomes, capital expenditure and revenue expenditure are duly adjusted in the current year. This concept is also known as "concept of continuity".

This concept recognises the assets and liabilities of the business on the basis of productivity and not on the basis of this current realisable values on the assumption that they will be disposed of. Since, they are held in a going concern for earning income and not for resale, there is no meaning in showing realisable values on the balance sheet.

3. Money measurement concept: Accounting records only those transactions which can be expressed in money value, i.e., monetary transactions. Transactions which cannot be expressed in terms of money do not find place in books of accounts though they may be useful for the business, tefficiency and loyalty of employees, e.g., integrity of management, etc.

Actually, the basic purpose of using money values is to implement an element of uniformity among diversity. Therefore, fixed assets like land, furniture are expressed in terms of money and not in terms of acres of land or number of furniture say 10 tables and 10 chairs, etc.

The major drawbacks of this concept are:

(1) It does not recognise the changes in purchase power of monetary unit, and

(2) It never accounts for qualitative factors such as human genius, which may be capable of being highly productive.

4. Cost concept: According to this concept:

(a) An asset is shown in the accounting records at the actual price paid for its acquisition and

(b) This cost is the basis for all subsequent accounting for assets. For instance, if an acre of land is purchased for Rs. 5,00,000 it would be recorded in books @ Rs. 00,000 even if the market value happens to be Rs. 7,00,000. Similarly, in case its value is reduced to Rs 4,00,000 after a year, it is continued to be shown at Rs. 5,00,000 only and not @ Rs. 4,00,000.

5. Accounting period concept: This concept provides for division of life of the business into appropriate segments for evaluating the results ot the business after each segment. Though the life of the business is indefinite (as per going concern concept), the assessment of income and financial position of the business after a very long period is not fair as it would not be helpful in taking proper corrective steps at appropriate time. Therefore, it is absolutely necessary that after each segment (period) or time interval the businessman must 'stop' and 'see back' what is happening. In accounting terminology, such segment or time interval is called 'accounting period', which is usually a year or 365 days or 12 months.

At the end of each accounting period profit and loss account and balance sheet is prepared. Profit and loss account discloses profit or loss made during the accounting period while the balance sheet exihibits the financial strength or weakness of the business on the last day of accounting.

6. Dual aspect concept: 'Every debit must have a corresponding credit' is the principle of dual aspect concept. Under this concept, the twofold aspects of each transaction (i.e., debit-receiving aspect and credit-giving aspect) are recorded.

For example, purchase of machinery for Rs. 1,00,000 is a transaction. Here, machinery account is debited with Rs. 1,00,000 as receiving aspect and cash account is credited with Rs. 1,00,000 as giving or outgoing aspect. This is nothing but double-entry principle.

This accounting equation, assets = equities (or liabilities + capital) is based on this concept.

7. Matching concept: The process of relating cost to revenue is called matching process or concept. This concept is based on accounting period concept. Income made during the period can be measured only when the revenue is earned during the period is compared with expenditure incurred for earning that revenue. The question when the payment was received or made is irrelevant.

It should be noted that:

1. Cost of fixed assets should not be taken but only depreciation on such assets related to that accounting period is taken for matching purpose
2. Prepaid expenses are excluded from total costs and
3. Outstanding expenses must be included (added) to total cost.

8. Realisation concept: Under this concept revenue is recognised only after the sale is made. In other words, revenue realised (either by sale of goods or rendering services) during an accounting period should only be taken to income statement/ Pg/account. Unearned or unrealised revenue should not be taken into account.

Examples

1. When goods are sold to customers, they are liable to pay for the goods as soon as property in goods is transferred from seller to buyer. Therefore, it is considered revenue earned;
2. When an order is received for goods from a customer, it does not mean that revenue is earned or realised;
3. Similarly, when an advance payment is made by the buyer the same cannot be treated as revenue realised, unless the entire price for goods is paid and ownership goods is passed on from the seller to the buyer.

9. Verifiable and objective evidence concept: Verifiability and objectivity imply reliability, trustworthiness, dependability which are very useful for conveying accounting data and information furnished in periodical accounting statements and reports. There should always be some documentary evidence for establishing the truth reflected in the said reports or statements. Entries which are recorded in accounting from transactions and data reported in financial statements must be based on objectively determined evidence.

In short, there should be no entry without documentary evidence and there should be no documentary evidence without an entry. Then only it is possible to retain the confidence of users of financial statement. It will minimise the chances of errors and frauds.

Invoices, and vouchers for purchases and sales, and expenses physical checking of stock on hand are examples of objective evidence which are capable of verification.

10. Accrual concept: This requires the recognition of both revenue as well as expenses. According to this concept, all expenses and incomes accrued (i.e., falling due) in one accounting year in which they are spent or earned, must be taken into account for determining profit or loss, which indicates that income earned, though not received in that year must be added to profit and the expenses incurred through not paid in that year should be deducted from profit. Similarly, income received in advance must be deducted from the concerned item of income and expenses prepared must be deducted from the concerned item of income and expense before ascertaining the profit or loss.

In short, the outcome of this concept is that if the capital at the end of the year is in excess of capital at the beginning of the year, there is profit or vice versa.

(b) Conventions

The term 'convention' signifies a customs or tradition followed in the preparation of accounting statments. The following are the accounting conventions.

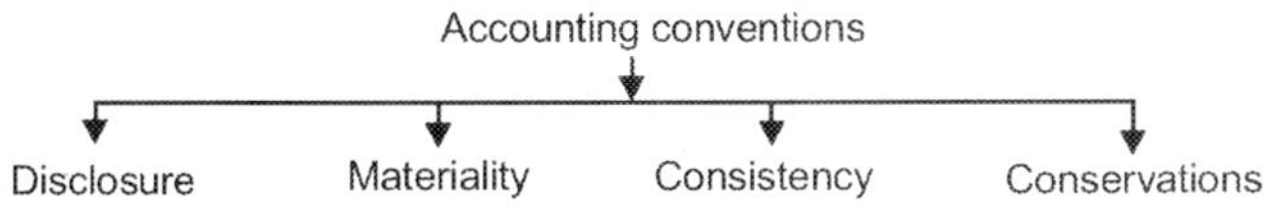

1. Convention of disclosure: The doctrine of disclosure requires honest preparation of financial statement and for this purpose, all the significant information should be disclosed. Financial statements are prepared to convey accounting information to the various parties who are interested in it—shareholders, investors, creditors, government etc. As such the significant information such as basis for valuation of fixed assets, investments, closing stock, etc., should be made clearly in the balance sheet.

This convention is gives more importance to the Peculiar feature of company form of organisation where there is separation of ownership from management and more so, the Companies Act, 1956, has made proper provisions for disclosure of essential information relating to accounting data, where the concealment of material information is limited in particular.

2. Convention of materiality: Materiality means 'relative importance'. An item or transaction should be regarded a material if there is a reason to believe that the knowledge of it would influence the decision of investors. On the other hand, an item is regarded a immaterial or insignificant if it is found that it is not so significant to influence the quality of financial statements or the decision of investors.

In short, the principle of materiality implies that the transactions that have immaterial or insignificant effects should not be recorded and reported in financial statements. It is for an accountant, to decide what is material and what is immaterial. Materiality (significance) or otherwise impact a transaction can be decided in terms of its on financial position, results of operations and on evaluation made by the users.

3. Convention of consistency: This doctrine requires continuous application and observation of accounting rules, practices and principles. It means, there should not be frequent changes in the application of accurate rules and principles. This is necessary to move the comparison make on of fiancial statements of different periods, meaningful and decisions based on such comparison one appropriate.

This principle helps to eliminate personal bias of the accountants since he is not allowed to change any accounting method or principle according to his own opionion and to prepare a periodical financial statement which is more dependable, reliable and comparable.

4. Convention of conservation (prudence): This principle implies policy of cautions or playing safe and had its origin as 'safeguard against possible losses in a world of uncertainity'. This principle is often described as 'anticipate no profit and provide for all possible losses.

According to this principle all losses that have occurred or likely to occur must be recognised but does not account for gains unless and until they are actually realised. Provision for doubtful debts, provision for discount on debtors, provision for fluctuation in the prices of investments is made on account of this connention. Again, it is because of this principle that the stock (inventory) is always valued at cost price or market price whichever is less and the intangible assets like goodwill, patents, trademarks, etc., are written off.

The significance of this principle is that the profit and loss account should indicate true and fair view of profit or loss and balance sheet should exihibit true and fair view of financial position.

1.14 BRANCHES OF ACCOUNTING

The following are the different branches of accounting:

1. Financial Accouting: This branch of accounting mainly is concerned with recording to the transactions which can b expressed on monetory values with a view to ascertain profit or loss during a partrental accounting period, to ascertain the financial strength or weakness of the business and to excercise control over property of every kind belonging to the business.

2. Cost Accounting: This branch of accounting is mainly concerned with ascertainment of cost of a product and to proper control over the costs to be incurred. Ascertainment of cost per unit of product enables the management to determine price of a product and profit margin per unit of product. Hence, the cost accounting techniques are useful for management on performing managerial functions effectively.

3. Management Accounting: This branch of accounting is mainly concerned with application of accounting technique for providing information useful to the management at various levels, in effective discharge managerial functions such as:—planning, decision making and controlling various activities of the firm.

2

Conversion of Single Entry to Double Entry

2.1 INTRODUCTION

Any system of accounting that does not recognise both debit and credit aspects of each and every transaction relating to a business enterprise is called the incomplete or single entry system. In contrast to this, the system of accounting the principle of which is 'every debit must have corresponding credit' is called the double entry system.

2.2 MEANING OF SINGLE ENTRY

A business enterprise is said to be using single entry system, if it does not follow the principles of *double entry system* of bookkeeping completely. In other words, the act of recording only one aspect of transaction may be debit or credit, in accordance with convenience of a trader called single entry system of bookkeeping.

Therefore, single entry system is also called '*incomplete, inaccurate, unscientific and unsystematic* method of recording transactions.

2.3 PECULIAR FEATURES OF THE SINGLE ENTRY SYSTEM

The following are the peculiar features of the single entry system:

1. For some transactions involving personal accounts, both the aspects of transaction are recorded. For example, (1) when cash is received from customers, it is recorded both in customer's account and also in cash account (cash account Dr, To customer's account) (2) Similarly, for payment of cash to creditors, is recorded both in creditor's account and also in cash account (creditor's account Dr, To cash account).
2. For some transactions involving impersonal accounts, only one aspect is recorded, e.g., cash purchases, cash sales, expenses paid, incomes received, purchase of fixed assets etc., where cash paid or received only is recorded.
3. For some other transactions, no entry is made in the books of accounts, such as depreciation provided on fixed assets, provision for doubtful debts or bad debts etc.

   For this reason, the single entry system is also called mixture of double entry, single entry and no entry method of recording business transactions.

2.4 DEFINITION OF SINGLE ENTRY

In his *Dictionary of Accountants*, Kohlers defines 'single entry' as:
'A system of book-keeping in which as a rule only records cash and personal accounts are maintained. It is always an incomplete double entry, varying with circumstances".

2.5 SALIENT FEATURES OF THE SINGLE ENTRY SYSTEM

The important characteristic features of the single entry system are:

1. Maintenance of personal accounts: For the transaction involving personal accounts—debtors and creditors, both aspects of transaction are recorded. For instance, for cash received from customers, it is recorded both in cash account and the personal account of the customer.

2. Maintenance of cash book: For the transactions involving impersonal accounts—expenses incurred, incomes received, purchase of assets etc., only reciept or payment of cash is recorded.

3. No uniformity: The system of recording transactions vary from firm to firm, as the transactions are recorded as per the need or convenience of the trader.

4. All accounts are not maintained: Under this system, generally, the personal accounts of debtors and creditors and cash account are maintained. Real accounts other than cash account and nominal accounts do not find place.

5. Nature: It is an incomplete, inaccurate, unscientific and unsystematic method of recording business transactions.

6. Suitability: This system is best suited for small business enterprises like sole trading concerns and a few partnership firms.

2.6 ADVANTAGES OF THE SINGLE ENTRY SYSTEM

1. Simple method: It is a very simple method of recording transactions.

2. Economical: It is less costlier, because, very few books of accounts are maintained under this system.

3. Suitability: It is best suited for small business concerns, where the number of transactions to be recorded are less and have a few assets and liabilities.

4. Knowledge of principles of bookkeeping: It does not require knowledge of principles of bookkeeping to record the transaction.

2.7 DRAWBACKS OF THE SINGLE ENTRY SYSTEM

1. Nature: It is an incomplete, in accurate, unscientific and unsystematic method of recording transactions.

2. Preparation of trial balance: As twofold aspects of a transaction are not recorded, it is impossible to prepare trial balance.

3. Arithmetical accuracy: As the trial balance cannot be prepared, it is impossible to check the arithmetical accuracy of accounts.

4. Much scope for errors and frauds: As the arithmetical accuracy of accounts cannot be checked, there is much scope for errors and frauds to creep into the books of account.

5. Does not reveal true profit: In the absence of nominal accounts—sales, purchases, expeses, incomes, etc., it is not possible to determine the correct profit or loss.

6. Impossible to judge the correct financial status: In the absence of real accounts—accounts of properties of business, if is not possible to evaluate financial strength or weakness of a business enterprise.

7. Goodwill of the business cannot be determined: Due to incomplete system of recording business transactions, it is impossible to value the goodwill of the firm in the event of purchase or sale of business.

8. Cannot be produced as evidence: The financial statements prepared under this sytem are not accepted as evidence by the courts because the information provided is unreliable.

9. Difficult to compute insurance claim: In case of loss or damage to goods, amount of claim to be lodged with insurance company cannot be ascertained correctly due to incomplete records.

10. Computation of purchase consideration: It is difficult to compute purchase consideration in case of sale of business under this system of accounting.

1.8 TYPES OF SINGLE ENTRY

Based on the books of accounts maintained, the single entry system can be divided into three categories, namely:

1. Pure single entry system: Is one under which only the personal accounts of debtors and creditors are maintained.

2. Simple single entry system: Is one under which apart from maintaining the personal accounts of debtors and creditors, a cash book, i.e., a principal subsidiary book is maintained.

3. Quasi single entry system: Is one under which, apart from maintaining personal accounts of debtors and creditors, a cash book and a few other subsidiary books like purchase book, sales book, purchase returns, book, sales return book, etc., are maintained.

1.9 DOUBLE ENTRY AND SINGLE ENTRY—DISTINCTION

Points of Difference	Double entry system	Single entry systm
1. Nature	Is complete, accurate, scientific and systematic system of recording transactions	Is incomplete, inaccurate, unscientific and unsystematic method of recording transactions
2. Meaning	Twofold aspects of each and every transaction (i.e., both debit and credit aspects) are recorded.	Only one aspect of the transaction, may be debit or credit is recorded as per the convenience of the trader.

(Contd.)

(Contd.)

3.	Maintenance of accounts	All accounts, namely, personal accounts, real accounts and nominal accounts are maintained	Only personal accounts of debtors and creditors and a cash book are maintained.
4.	Preparation of trial balance	Trial balance can be prepared	Trial balance cannot be prepared
5.	Checking of airthmetical accuracy of accounts	Is possible	Is impossible
6.	Preparation of profit and loss account	In the presence of nominal accounts trading and profit and loss account can be prepared and correct profit or loss can be determined.	In the absence of nominal accounts, trading and profit and loss account cannot be prepared and correct profit/ loss cannot be determined.
7.	Ascertainment of true financial position	In the presence of real accounts balance sheet can be prepared and correct financial position can be ascertained.	In the absence of real accounts balance sheet cannot be prepared and it is impossible to ascertain true financial position.
8.	Chances of errors and frauds	As it is possible to check airthmetical accuracy of accounts, there is limited scope for errors and frauds to to creep into books of accounts.	As it is impossible to check the arithmatical accuracy of accounts, there is much scope for erros and frauds.
9.	Cost involved	This system necessiates maintenance of large number of books of accounts. Therefore it is costly	This system requires maintenance of only personal accounts of debtors and creditors. Therefore, it is economical.
10.	Suitability	Best suited for medium sized and big business enterprises	Best suited for small business organisations like sole trading concerns and for small partnership firms.
11.	Legal evidence	Accounts prepared under this system are accepted as legal evidence by the courts.	Accounts prepared under this system are not accepted by the court as legal evidence.
12.	Comparability	Accounts prepared under double entry system are comparable because definite rules and procedures are followed in preparation of accounts	Accounts prepared under the single entry system are not comparable because no definate rules or procedures are followed in the preparation of such accounts

(Contd.)

(Contd.)

13. Recognition	Accounts prepared under this system are recognised by taxation authorities	Accounts prepared under this system are not recognised by taxation authorities.
14. Purchase consideration	Purchase consideration can be ascertained easily in the event of sale or purchase of business.	Purchase consideration cannot be ascertained because accounts prepared under this system are unreliable.

2.10 METHODS OF CALCULATING PROFIT OR LOSS UNDER THE SINGLE ENTRY SYSTEM

There are two methods of calculating profit or loss under the single entry system, namely,

(a) Statement of affairs method (or) net worth method, and

(b) Conversion of single entry into double entry.

2.10.1 Statement of Affairs Method

Under the single entry system profit or loss cannot be ascertained by preparing trading and profit and loss account as in the case of double entry system. However, the business results can be determined by comparing capital at the beginning and at the end of the accounting year. Excess of closing capital over opening capital is considered profit or otherwise loss.

Capital both at the beginning and at the end of accounting year is ascertained by preparing "Statement of affairs" for the respective periods, taking into consideration assets and liabilities at the begining and end of the accounting year. Capitals so calculated will be compared and thereby increase in capital is considered profit and decrease in capital loss.

However, the following factors affecting the capital should also be considered to determine current profit or loss such as:

1. Withdrawals made during the year
2. Interest on capital and drawings
3. Depreciation on fixed assets
4. Additional capital introduced during the year.
5. Expenses paid and to be paid. (outstanding)
6. Incomes received and to be received (accrued)
7. Prepaid expenses and
8. Pre-received incomes.

Distinction between statement of affairs and balance sheet

	Points of difference	Balance sheet	Statement of affairs
1.	Preparation	Balance sheet is prepared under the double entry system.	Prepared under single entry system.
2.	Source	Values of assets and liabilities shown in the balance sheet are drawn from ledger accounts	Values of assets and liabilities shown in this statement are partly drawn from ledger account partly by inspection and partly from the memory.
3.	Object	The main objective of preparing a balance sheet is to ascertain financial strength or weakness of the business	The main objective is to ascertain opening or closing capital.
4.	Tracing of ommisions	Omission of an asset or liability can be traced easily	Cannot be traced easily because the statement is not prepared from ledger balances.
5.	Reliability	Information disclosed by a balance sheet is reliable and dependable.	Infromation disclosed by the statement of affairs is unreliable and not dependable.

2.10.2 Conversion Method

The single entry system is an incomplete, inaccurate, unscientific and unsystematic method of recording business transactions. It has to be converted into double-entry to make if a complete, accurate, scientific and systematic method of recording transactions. More so, when profit or loss were to be ascertained by preparing *Trading and profit and loss account as in case double-entry*, it becomes necessary to convert single entry into double entry.

(a) Objectives of Conversion

1. To overcome the defects of the single entry system.
2. To have complete record of transactions
3. To ascertain correct profit or loss
4. To ascertain true and fair financial position
5. To provide ideal and reliable accounting information
6. To maintain accuracy of books of accounts
7. To avoid chances of erros and frauds.

(b) Steps in conversion single entry into double entry

In the light of information required for preparation of trading and profit and loss account and balance sheet we should know the information readily available and information missing or hidden, in the given problem. Thereafter, we should follow the following steps in converting single entry into double entry.

Firstly, prepare *opening statement of affairs* to find out the opening capital, where such capital is always equal to the excess of assets over liabilities at beginning of the accounting year.

Secondly, prepare *Summary of cash book* with the given receipts and payments of cash and ascertain opening or closing cash balance as the case may be. Summary of cash book also enables us to identify cash purchases, cash sales, drawings, direct and indirect expenses incurred and incomes (if any received.)

Thirdly, the following equations may be adopted to ascertain missing items like:

Cost of sales: opening stocks + purchases – closing stock and

Purchases: cost of sales + closing stock – opening stocks

Lastly, the following accounts are to be prepared to ascertain relevant missing items depending upon the circumstances of a case.

1. **Total debtors' account:** This account is required to be prepared to ascertain any one of the four items giving below:
   (a) Opening debtors
   (b) Closing debtors
   (c) Cash received from debtors
   (d) Credit sales.

Proforma of Total Debtor Account

Dr. Cr.

Particulars	Amount (₹)	Particulars	Amount (₹)
To opening balance b/d	xxx	By cash A/c	xxx
To credit sales	xxx	By bank A/c	xxx
To bills receivable dishonoured	xxx	By bills receivable A/c	xxx
To interest on overdue accounts	xxx	By sales returns or returns inwards A/c	xxx
		By discount allowed	xxx
		By bad debts	xxx
		By allowances	xxx
		By Balance c/d	xxx
	xxx		xxx

2. **Bills receivable account:** This account is prepared to ascertain any one of the four items given below:
   (a) Opening bills receivable
   (b) Closing bills receivable
   (c) Cash received against B/R
   (d) B/R received from debtors

Proforma of Bills Receivable Account

Dr. Cr.

Particulars	Amount (₹)	Particulars	Amount (₹)
To opening balance B/d	xxx	By cash/bank a/c	xxx
To Debtors A/c		By debtors A/c	
(B/R received from Dr)	xxx	(B/R dishonoured)	xxx
		By closing balance a/c	xxx
	xxx		xxx

3. **Total creditor account:** This account is prepared to ascertain any one of the four items given below:
(a) Opening creditors,
(b) Closing creditors
(c) Cash paid to creditors
(d) Credit purchases

Proforma of Total Creditor Account

Dr. Cr.

Particulars	Amount (₹)	Particulars	Amount (₹)
To Cash A/c	xxx	By opening balance B/d	xxx
To Bank A/c	xxx	By credit purchase A/c	xxx
To B/P issued A/c	xxx	By B/P dishonoured A/c	xxx
To return outwards A/c	xxx		
or			
Purchase returns A/c	xxx		
To discount received A/c	xxx		
To allowance A/c	xxx		
To closing balance c/d	xxx		
	xxx		xxx

4. **Bills payable account:** This account is prepared to ascertain any one of the four items given below:
(a) Opening bills payable,
(b) Closing bills payable,
(c) Cash paid against bills payable
(d) B/p issued to creditors

Proforma of Bills Payable Account

Dr. Cr.

Particulars	Amount (₹)	Particulars	Amount (₹)
To Cash A/c	xxx	By opening balance B/d	xxx
To Bank A/c	xxx	By creditors	xxx
To Crditors A/c	xxx	(Bills payable issued	
(B/P dishonoured)		to creditors)	
To closing balance c/d	xxx		
	xxx		xxx

Problems and Solutions

Illustration 1: From the following particulars Mr. Ananth, who keeps his books under the single entry system, ascertain the total sales.

	(₹)
Opening stock	36,000
Purchases	1,80,000
Wages	21,000
Closing stock	45,000

Rate of gross profit $33\text{-}^1/_3$ on sales

(B.U. 2nd Sem. B.Com June 2005)

Solution: Working Notes: (a) Profit on cost = ?

$33\text{-}^1/_3$ on sales mean $\frac{33^1/_3}{100}$ i.e., 1/3.

Here, sales are given. However, cost of goods sold can be ascertained.

∴ Let us find out profit on cost

Cost = sales – gross profit

$66\text{-}^2/_3 = 100 - 33\text{-}^1/_3$

$\therefore$ Profit on cost = $\frac{33\text{-}^1/_3}{66\text{-}^2/_3}$ i.e., $^1/_2$

(b) Cost of goods sold = ?

Cost of goods sold = opening stock + purchase + wages – closing stock

= 36,000 + 1,80,000 + 21,000 – 45,000

∴ Cost of goods sold = ₹ 1,92,000

(c) Profit on cost = ?

$$\text{Cost of goods sold} \times \frac{33\text{-}^1/_3}{66\text{-}^2/_3} \text{ or } \frac{1}{2}$$

$$\therefore \quad 1,92,000 \times -\frac{1}{2}$$

= 96,000

(d) Total sales = ?

Total sales = cost of sales + G/P

= 1,92,000 + 96,000

∴ Sales = 2,88,000

Illustration 2: From the following details drawn from the books of Naija, you are required to ascertain the opening stock.

	(₹)
Purchases made during the year	22,000
Sales made during the year	33,000
Closing stock	2,000
Wages, freight	500
Indirect expenses	700
Rate of gross profit on cost	1/2
Returns in wards	3,000
Returns outwards	2,000

(B.U. 2nd Sem. B.Com. 2009 June)

Solution: *Working Notes: (1) Rate G/P* on *Sales = ?*
In this problem, rate of G/P on cost is given and on sales are not given. Therefore, G/P on cost should be converted into G/P on sales as follows:

When cost is ₹ 100. Profit is $\frac{1}{2}$ i.e., $100 \times \frac{1}{2} = 50$

$$\therefore \text{ profit on cost} = \frac{50}{100} \text{ or } \frac{1}{2}$$

Sales = cost + profit

150 = 100 + 50

$$\text{Gross profit on sales} = \frac{50}{150} \text{ or } \frac{1}{3} \text{ or } \frac{50}{150} \times 100 = 33\frac{1}{3}\%$$

(2) Opening stock: To ascertain the opening stock, memorandum trading A/c is to prepared as follows:

(3) Indirect expenses: Should be ignored because it is given just for the information. These expenses are shown in profit and loss account.

Memorandam Trading A/c
For the year ending ________

Dr. Cr.

Particulars		Amount (₹)	Particulars		Amount (₹)
To opening stock (Balancing figure)		1,500	By sales	33,000	
			Un: returns in wards	3,000	30,000
To purchases	22,000				
less retuns outwards	2,000	20,000	By closing stock		2,000
To wages, freight		500			
To gross profit (1/2 × 3,000)		10,000			
		32,000			32,000

Problem 3: From the information given below, prepare total debtor and bills receivable A/c and ascertain missing returns.

Total debtors on 1-1-2011	15,000
Total debtors on 31.12.2011	18,000
Bills receivable on 1-1-2011	7,500
Bills receivable on 31-12-2011	9,000
Transactions made during the year 2011:	
Cash received from debtors	45,000
Cash received against B/R	35,250
Bad debts	900
Discount allowed to customers	2100
B/R dishonoured	750
Returns towards	3,000

Solution 3: *Working Notes:*

(1) Relating to Dr A/c : opening debtors closing debtors and cash received from debtors are given in the problem ∴ missing itme is '*credit sales*'

(2) Relating to B/R A/c: Opening B/R, closing B/R and cash receivedd against B/R are given ∴ '*B/R recieved from debtors* is missing.

(1) Ascertainment of credit sales:

Total Debtors A/c

Dr. Cr.

Particulars	Amount (₹)	Particulars	Amount (₹)
To balance B/d 1.1.11 To credit sales (Bal. fig.) To B/r dishonoured A/c	15,000 90,750 750	By cash a/c By bills receivable A/c By sales returns By bad debts By discount By balance cld 31.12.11	45,000 37,500 3,000 900 2,100 18,000
	1,06,500		1,06,500

(2) Ascertainment of B/R received from debtors:

Bills Receivable A/c

Dr. Cr.

Particulars	Amount (₹)	Particulars	Amount (₹)
To balance B/d 1.1.11	7,500	By Cash A/c	35,250
To debtors A/c—B/R received from debtors.	37,500	By Debtors A/c (B/R dishonoured)	750
(Balancing figure)		By balance closed 31.12.11	9,000
	45,000		45,000

Illustration 4: Prepare total creditors account and bills payable account from the information given below and ascertain the missing information.

	₹
Total creditors on 1.1.2011	11,000
Total creditors on 31.12.2011	12,000
Bills payable on 1.1.2011	3,000
Bills payable on 31.12.2011	4,500

Transactions made during the year were:

Payments to creditors	42,000
Returns outwards	2,500
Cash paid against bills payable	16,800
B/P dishonoured	500
Discount received from creditors	1,100

Solution: *Working notes:*

(1) Relating total creditors A/c—opening creditors, closing creditors and cash paid to creditors are given. ∴ *Credit Purchases* is missing

(2) Relating to bills payable A/c—Opening B/P, closing B/P, cash paid against B/P, are given. ∴ B/P issued to creditors is not given

(1) Ascertainment of credit purchases:

Total Creditors A/c

Dr. Cr.

Particulars	Amount (₹)	Particulars	Amount (₹)
To cash a/c	42,000	By balance B/d 1.1.11	11,000
To B/P issued a/c.	18,800	By credit purchases a/c	64,900
To discount earned	1,100	(Balance figure)	
To returns outwards	2,500	By B/P dishonoured a/c	500
To balance closed 31.12.11	12,000		
	76,400		76,400

(2) Ascertainment B/P issued to creditors:

Bills Payable A/c

Dr. Cr.

Particulars	Amount (₹)	Particulars	Amount (₹)
To cash a/c	16,800	By Balance B/d 1.1.11	3,000
To Creditors (B/P dishonoured	500	By Creditors a/c.	18,800
To Balance closed 31.12.11	4,500	(B/P issued - Bal. fig.)	
	21,800		21,800

Illustration 5: From the following information, calculate the total sales:

	₹
Opening balance of debtors	30,800
B/R at the beginning	7,800
B/R encashed during the year	20,900
Cash received from debtors	70,000
Bad debts written off	2,800
Returns inwards	8,700
B/a dishonoured	1,800
B/a at the end of the year	6,000
Debtors at the end of the year	25,500
Cash sales as per cash book	40,900

(B.U. 2nd Sem. B.Com., June 2006)

Solution *Working Notes:*

(1) Total sales: cash sales + credit sales
Cash sales is given in the problem and credit sales is not given. Hence, *credit sales* is to be ascertained by preparing total debtors' account.

(2) Opg, B/R, clg, B/R and cash received against B/R is given but' B/R *received from debtors*' is not given. Hence, the same has to be ascertained by preparing B/R a/c.

(1) Ascertainment of credit sales:

Total Debtors' Account

Dr. Cr.

Particulars	Amount (₹)	Particulars	Amount (₹)
To opening balance B/d	30,800	By cash a/c	70,000
To credit sale a/c	95,300	By B/R a/c.	20,900
(Balance figure)		By returns inwards a/c	8,700
To B/R dishonoured a/c	1,800	By bad debts a/c	2,800
		By closing balance c/d	25,500
	1,28,900		1,27,900

(2) B/R received from debtors:

Bills receivale A/c

Dr. Cr.

Particulars	Amount (₹)	Particulars	Amount (₹)
To opening balance B/d	7,800	By cash a/c	20,900
To debtors A/c (B/R received from debtors - bal. fig.).	20,900	By Debtors a/c (B/r dishonoured)	1,800
		By closing balance c/d	6,000
	28,700		28,700

(3) Total sales: cash sales + credit sales ∴ 40900 + 95300 = ₹ 1,36,200

Illustration 6: Prepare total debtors a/c and B/R a/c for the year ending 31.3.2011 from the following details:

	₹
Total sales during the year	1,12,500
Cash sales during the year	29,450
Returns inwards	450
Discount allowed	150
Cash received from debtors	69,400
Cash received against B/R	2,900
Debtors on 1-4-2010	39,250
Debtors on 31-3-2011	49,850
B/R on 1-4-2010	1,900
B/R on 31-3-2011	1,450

(B.U. 2nd Sem. B. Com., June 2007)

Solution:

Working notes:

(1) In this problem all information relating to total debtors' account is given. Credit sales = Total sales – cash sales.

(2) But *B/R receivable received from debtors* is not given ∴ the same has to be ascertained by preparing B/R a/c.

Total Debtors' Account

Dr. Cr.

Particulars	Amount (₹)	Particulars	Amount (₹)
To opening balance B/d (1.4.10)	39,250	By cash A/c	69,400
To credit sales A/c (1,12,500–29,450)	83,050	By bills Receivable A/c.	2,450
		By returns inwards A/c	450
		By discount A/c	150
		By balance c/d 31.3.2011	49,850
	1,22,300		1,22,300

(2) B/R received from Debtors = ?

Bills Receivable Account

Dr. Cr.

Particulars	Amount	Particulars	Amount
To Balance B/d 1.4.10	1,900	By Cash A/c	2,900
To Debtors A/c (B/R received from debtors – Balancing. fixture)	2,450	By Debtors A/c (B/R dishonoured)	-NIL
		By Balance c/d 31.3.11	1,450
	4,350		4,350

Illustration 7: From the following details available, you are required to determine total purchases for the year 2011.

	₹
Total creditors on 1.1.2011	58,800
Bills payable on 1.1.2011	14,020
Discount received from creditors	2,180
Cash purchases made during the year	7,200
Cash paid to creditors (including ₹ 2,700, a payment to suppliers of furniture on credit)	35,240
Return outwards	1,750
Bills payable on 31-12-2012	21,520
Payments against bills payable	20,000
B/R endorsed to creditors	3,090
Total creditors balance on 31-12-2011	44,650

(B.U. 1994 modified)

Solution: Working Notes:

(1) Total purchases = cash purchases + credit purchases

(2) Here credit purchases are not given. ∴ Same is to be ascertained by preparing total creditors' A/c.

(3) Here, total creditors means total trade creditors. Non-trade creditors do not find place in total creditors A/c. Hence, such non-trade creditors should be eliminated.

	₹
As such, payments to creditors as given	35,240
Less: Payment to suppliers of furniture	2,700
Actual payments to trade creditors	32,540

(4) B/P issued to creditors is not given. Hence, the same is ascertained by preparing bills payable A/c.

1. Ascertainment of Total purchases:

Total purchases = Cash purchases + credit purchases

= 7,200 + 52,910

Total purchases ₹ **60,110**

2. Ascertainment of credit purchases:

Total Creditor A/c

Dr. Cr.

	₹		₹
To cash A/c	32,540	By balance B/d 1.1.11	58,800
To Bills payable A/c	27,500	By credit purchases	52,910
By Discount received A/c	2,180	(Balancing figure)	
By Returns outwards A/c	1,750		
By B/R endorsed A/c	3,090		
By balance c/d	44,650		
	1,11,710		1,11,710

3. Ascertainment B/P issued to creditors:

Bills Payable A/c

Dr. Cr.

	₹		₹
By cash A/c	20,000	By balance B/d 1.1.11	14,020
By creditors (B/P dishonoured)	NIL	By creditors A/c (B/P issued	
By balance c/d 31.12.11	21,520	to as balance figure).	27,500
	41,520		41,520

Problem 8: From the following information ascertain The 'Total Sales' and 'Total purchases'

Balance on	1.4.2011	31.3.2012
	₹	₹
Sundry debtors	65,000	72,000
Bills receivable	37,000	30,000
Sundry creditors	48,000	50,000
Bills payable	24,000	21,000

Transactions made during the year 2011-12.

	₹
Cash sales	38,750
Cash received from debtors	1,62,500
Discount allowed to customers	4,500
Returns inwards	12,000
Returns outwards	2,500
Cash received against B/R	58,000
Cash paid against B/P	40,000
Cash purchases	25,000
Cash paid to creditors	1,07,500
Bad debts written-off	5,000

(B.U. Nov. 1991, Nov. 1997)

Solution: Working Capital:

(1) Total sales = cash sales + credit sales

2) Total purchases = cash purchases + credit purchases

(3) Credit sales are not given ∴ The same is ascertained, preparing total debtors A/c.

(4) B/R received from debtors is missing ∴ The same is ascertained, preparing B/R A/c.

(5) Ascertainment of credit purchases:

Total Creditors' Account

Dr. Cr.

	₹		₹
To cash A/c	1,07,500	By balance B/d 1.4.11	48,000
To bills payable.	37,000	By credit purchases	1,49,000
To returns outwards	2,500	(Balancing figure)	
To balance c/d 31.3.12	50,000		
	1,97,000		1,97,000

(6) Ascertainment of B/P isued of creditors:

Bills Payable A/c

Dr. Cr.

	₹		₹
To cash A/c	40,000	By balance B/d 1.4.11	24,000
To creditors (B/P dishonoured)	NIL	By creditors (B/P reused)	37,000
To balance old 31.3.12	21,000	(Balancing figure).	
	61,000		61,000

Problems and Solutions – Preparation of Trading and Profit & Loss a/c and Balance Sheet

Illustration 9: Sri Ganesh furnishes the following details for 2011-12.

Details	1.4.11	31.3.12
	₹	₹
Fixed assets	10,000	12,500
Debtors	12,500	20,000
Creditor	7,500	10,000
Stocks	5,000	7,500
Cash at bank	2,500	4,000

Additional information:	₹
Receipts from customers	1,25,000
Payments to suppliers	1,00,000
Discounts allowed by suppliers	2,500
Bad debts written off	3,500
Sundry expenses paid	15,000
Drawings made during the year	3,000
Cash sales	2,500
Cash purchases	5,500
Purchase return	13,000

Further: (i) Depreciate fixed assets @ 10%.

(ii) Provide for outstanding expenses ₹ 2,500

(iii) Provide a reserve for bad debts ₹ 1,200

Prepare: (a) Trading and profit and loss A/c for the year ended 31st March, 2012

(b) Balance sheet as on 31st March, 2012.

Solution: Working Notes:

(1) Before we proceed with preparation of final accounts we should ascertain the missing information. Therefore, let us list out missing items, namely:
(1) Credit sales (2) Credit purchases

(2) There is increase in the value of fixed assets on 31.3.12 by ₹ 2,500 (i.e., 12,500 – 10,000), may be due to purchase of fixed assets during the year. Date of purchase is not given, hence, it is assumed that they are purchased at the beginning of the year itself, for calculating depreciation.

3) Opening capital is missing. It is to be ascertained by preparing opening statement of affairs.

(1) Ascertainment of credit sales

Total Debtors' A/c

Dr. Cr.

Particulars	Amount (₹)	Particulars	Amount (₹)
To balance B/d 1.4.11	12,500	By cash A/c	1,25,000
To credit sales (Balancing figure)	1,36,000	To bad debts	3,500
		To balance c/d (31.3.12)	20,000
	1,48,500		1,48,500

(2) Ascertainment of credit purchases

Total Creditors' A/c

Dr. Cr.

Particulars	Amount (₹)	Particulars	Amount (₹)
To cash A/c	1,00,000	By balance B/d 1.4.11	7,500
To purchase returns	13,000	By credit purchases (Balancing figure)	1,18,000
To discount received	2,500		
To balance old 31.3.12	10,000		
	1,25,500		1,25,500

(3) Ascertainment of opening capital

Statement of affairs as on 01.4.11

Dr. Cr.

Liabilities	(₹)		(₹)
Capital (being excess of assets over liabilities)	22,500	Fixed assets	10,000
Creditors	7,500	Debtors	12,500
		Stocks	5,000
		Cash at bank	2,500
	30,000		30,000

Trading and Profit and Loss A/c
For the year ended 31st March, 2012

Dr. Cr.

Particulars		(₹)			(₹)
To opening stocks		5,000	By Sales:		
To Purchases: Cash	5,500		Cash	2,500	
+ Credit	1,18,000		+ Credit	1,36,000	
	1,23,500				1,38,500
Less: Purchase returns	13,000	1,10,500	To closing stocks		7,500
To gross profit c/d		30,500			
		1,46,000			1,46,000
To Sundry expenses	15,000		By gross profit B/d		30,500
Add: O/s expenses	2,500	17,500	By discount received		2,500
To bad debts	3,500				
Add: New res.	1,200	4,700			
To depreciation @ 10%		1,250			
To net profit c/d-		9,550			
		33,000			33,000

Balance Sheet
as on 31st March, 2012

Liabilities	₹	₹	Assets	₹	₹
Opening capital	22,500		Fixed assets	10,000	
Add: Net profit earned	9,550		+ Purchased during the year	2,500	
	32,050			12,500	
Less: Drawings made during the year	3,000	29,050	Less: Depreciation @ 10%	1,250	11,250
O/S Sundry expenses		2,500	Sundry debtors	20,000	

(Contd.)

(Contd.)

Sundry creditors	10,000	Less: Res. For bad debts	1,200	18,800
		Stocks		7,500
		Cash at bank		4,000
	41,550			41,550

Note: Summary of cash transactions are given. Therefore, let us prepare cash book and confirm whether there is any difference or not.

Cash Book

Dr. Cr.

Receipts	₹	Payments	₹
To opening balance B/d	2,500	By fixed assets	
To cash sales	2,500	(12,500 – 10,500)	2,500
To debtors	1,25,000	To creditors	1,00,000
		To sundry expenses	15,000
		To drawings	3,000
		To cash purchases	5,500
		To balance c/d-	4,000
	1,30,000		1,30,000

(CASE OF NEW BUSINESS)

Illustration 10: On 1st January 2011, Sri Dhanesh commenced his business. During the year, the made the following deposits into the bank.

	₹
Capital introduced	50,000
Cash sales	64,000
Collection from debtors	68,250
Cash received against B/R	6,000

Payments made through the bank during the year:

	₹
Creditors	1,06,300
Staff salaries	9,000
Furniture 1.7.11	10,000
Bills payable	3,500
Rent	9,000
Drawings	12,000

Additional informational:

1) Gross profit @ 25% on sales which were uniform throughout the year.
2) O/S liabilities for salaries ₹ 3,000 and rent ₹ 3,000.
3) Discount allowed by creditors ₹ 1,750 and discount allowed to customers ₹ 2,450 and bad debts written-off ₹ 1,250.
4) B/R received during year ₹ 11,500 and B/P issued to creditors during the year amounted to ₹ 10,000.
5) Balances of debtors and creditors on 31-12-2011 were ₹ 7000 and ₹ 14,000 respectively.
6) Depreciate furniture at 10%.

Prepare: a) Trading and profit and loss A/c for year ending 31st Dec, 2011 and
b) Balance sheet as on that date.

Solution: Working Notes:

(1) Since it is a newly commenced business, the question of opening balances (i.e., on 1-1-2011) of the following items does not arise:
   (a) Opening stock
   (b) Debtors
   (c) Creditors
   (d) Bills receivable
   (e) Bills payable
   (f) Bank balance
(2) Following are the missing items to be ascertained before preparing final accounts, namely,
   (a) Credit sales
   (b) Credit purchases
   (c) Closing bills receivable
   (d) Closing bills payable
   (e) Closing bank balance
   (f) Closing stock

A. Ascertainment of credit sales:

Total Debtors' A/c

Dr. Cr.

Particulars	Amount (₹)	Particulars	Amount (₹)
To balance B/d 1-1-11	NIL	By Cash A/c	68,250
To credit Sales (Balancing figure)	90,450	By bills receivable A/c	11,500
		By discount allowed	2,450
		By bad debts	1,250
		By clg. balance c/d. 31-12-11	7,000
	90,450		90,450

B. Ascertainment of credit purchases:

Total Creditors' A/c

Dr. Cr.

	(₹)		(₹)
To cash A/c	1,06,300	By balance B/d 1-1-11	NIL
To bills payable A/c	10,000	By credit purchases	1,32,050
To discount received	1,750	(Balancing figure)	
To balance c/d 31-12-11	14,000		
	1,32,050		1,32,050

C. Ascertainment of Closing Bills Receivable:

Bills Receivable A/c

Dr. Cr.

	(₹)		(₹)
To balance B/d 1-1-11	NIL	By cash A/c	6,000
To debtors A/c (B/R received)	11,500	By balance c/d 31-12-11	5,500
	11,500		11,500

D. Ascertainment of Closing Bills payable:

Bills Payable A/c

Dr. Cr.

	(₹)		(₹)
To Cash A/c	3,500	By Balance B/d 1-1-11	-NIL-
To Balance c/d 31-12-11	6,500	By Creditors A/c (B/P issued)	10,000
	10,000		10,000

E. Ascertainment of Closing Balance of Bank A/c

Bank Account

Dr. Cr.

	(₹)		(₹)
To balance B/d 1-1-11	NIL	By creditors A/c	1,06,300
To capital A/c	50,000	By staff salary A/c	9,000
To cash sales A/c	64,000	By furniture (1-7-11) A/c	10,000
To debtors A/c	68,250	By bills payable A/c	3,500
To bills receivable A/c	6,000	By rent A/c	9,000
		By drawings A/c	12,000
		By balance c/d 31.12.11	38,450
	1,88,250		1,88,250

F. Closing Stock=? Trading and Profit and Loss A/c
For the year ended 31st December, 2011

		(₹)			(₹)
To opening stocks 1-1-11		NIL	By Sales:	₹	
To purchases		1,32,050	Cash	64,000	
			Credit	90,450	1,54,450
To gross profit c/d (25% on sales)		38,613	By closing sock (Bal. fig.)		16,213
		1,70,663			1,70,663
		₹			
To Staff Salaries	9,000		By Gross Profit B/d		38,613
Add: O/S Salary	3,000	12,000	By Discount received		1,750
To rent	9,000				
Add O/S salary	3,000	12,000			
To discount allowed		2,450			
To bad debts		1,250			
To depreciation on furniture		500			
$10,000 \times \frac{10}{100} \times \frac{6}{12}$					
To net profit c/d-		12,163			
		40,363			40,363

Balance Sheet
As on 31st December, 2011

Capital and liability		Amount (₹)	Assets and properties		Amount (₹)
	(₹)				
Opening capital	50,000		Furniture	10,000	
Add:- N/P made	12,163		Less: Depreciation	500	9,500
	62,163				
Less: Drawings	12,000	50,163	Bank balance		38,450
Sundry creditors		14,000	Stocks		16,213
Bills payable		6,500	Sundry debtors		7,000
O/s liabilities for: Rent	3,000		Bills receivable		5,500
staff salary	3,000	6,000			
		76,663			76,663

Illustration 11: Sri Rajiv does not maintain regular accounts. From the following information provided by him prepare trading and profit and loss account for the year ended 31st Dec, 2011 and also a balance sheet as on that date.

Balances on 1st Jan, 2011:

	₹
Cash in hand	4,000
Cash at bank	28,000
Sundry debtors	23,000
Sundry creditors	15,000
Stocks	35,000
Fixed assets	20,000

During the year creditors were paid ₹ 26,000 in cash and ₹ 1,55,000 by cheques. Debtors paid in cash ₹ 55,000 and paid ₹ 1,90,000 by crossed cheques. The balance on 31.12.2011: Debtors ₹ 27,000 and creditors ₹ 35,000.

All expenses chargeable to profit and loss account were disbursed by cheques, except petty expenses amounting to ₹ 7,500 paid in cash. Outstanding expenses at the close were ₹ 2,000.

Closing stock on 31st December 2011 was ₹ 75,000. Net profit for the year was ₹ 41,000 after allowing 10% depreciation on fixed assets.

Sri Rajiv's drawings during the year were ₹ 10,000 in cash and ₹ 14,000 by cheques.

(B.U. April 1991)

Solution: *Working Notes:*

Before we proceed with the preparation of final accounts, we should list out missing items and make out how to ascertain items:

Missing Items	*How to ascertain:*
(1) Opening capital	Prepare opening statement of affairs
(2) Credit sales	Prepare total debtors A/c
(3) Credit purchases	Prepare total creditors A/c
(4) Closing cash and bank balances	Prepare cash book with cash and Bank columns
(5) Expenses paid by cheque	Prepare profit and loss A/c

(1) Opening capital = ?

Statement of Affairs
as on 1st Jan, 2011

Liabilities	Amount (₹)	Assets	Amount (₹)
Sundry creditors	15,000	Cash in hand	4,000
Capital (being excess of assets over liabilities)	95,000	Cash at bank	28,000
		Sundry debtors	23,000
		Stocks	35,000
		Fixed assets	20,000
	1,10,000		1,10,000

(2) Credit Sales : ?

Total Debtor A/c

Dr. Cr.

	₹		₹
To Balance B/d	23,000	By cash A/c	55,000
To Credit Sales (Balancing figure)	2,49,000	By bank A/c	1,90,000
		By balance c/d	27,000
	2,72,000		2,72,000

(3) Credit purchases :-

Total Creditor A/c

Dr. Cr.

	₹		₹
To cash A/c	26,000	By balance B/d	15,000
To bank A/c	1,55,000	By credit purchases (Balancing figure)	2,01,000
To balance c/d	35,000		
	2,16,000		2,16,000

(4) Closing Balances of Cash and Bank : ?

Cash Book

Dr. Cr.

Receipts	Cash	Bank	Payments	Cash	Bank
	₹	₹		₹	₹
To balance B/d	4,000	28,000	By creditors	26,000	1,55,000
To debtors	55,000	1,90,000	By petty expenses	7,500	NIL
			By indirect expenses	NIL	35,500
			By drawings	10,000	14,000
			By balance c/d (Balancing figure)	15,500	13,500
	59,000	2,18,000		59,000	2,18,000

(5) Indirect expenses: Are expenses debited to P&L A/c only. It is stated in the problem that all expenses chargeable to P&L A/c were disbursed by cheques, amount of expenses is missing. Hence, the same should be calculated as follows:

(a) G/Ps ?

Memorandry Trading A/c

Dr. Cr.

	₹		₹
To opening stocks	35,000	By Sales (cr)	2,49,000
To purchase (credit)	2,01,000	By clg. Stocks	75,000
To G/P c/d (Balancing figure)	88,000		
	3,24,000		3,24,000

(6) Indirect expenses – expenses chargeable to P&L A/c = ?

		₹
Gross profit (as calculated)		88,000
Less: other expenses given:-	₹	
Petty expenses	7,500	
O/s expenses	2,000	
Depreciations @ 10% on fixed assets	2,000	11,500
		76,500
Less: Net profit as given in the problem		41,000
Indirect expenses		35,500

Trading and Profit and Loss A/c
for the year ended 31st December 2011

Dr. Cr.

Particulars	Amount (₹)	Particulars	Amount (₹)
To opening stock	35,000	By sales	2,49,000
To purchases	2,01,000	By closing stock	75,000
To gross profit c/d	88,000		
	3,24,000		3,24,000
To indirect expenses	35,500	By gross profit c/d	88,000
To petty expenses	7,500		
To O/s expenses	2,000		
To depreciation on fixed assets	2,000		
To net profit c/d	41,000		
	88,000		88,000

Balance Sheet
As on 31st December, 2011

Liabilities		₹	Assets		₹
Sundry creditors		35,000	Cash in hand		15,500
O/s expenses		2,000	Cash at bank		13,500
	₹				
Opening capital	95,000		Closing stock		75,000
Add: Net profit	41,000		Sundry Debtors		27,000
	1,36,000		Fixed Assets	2,000	20,000
Less: Drawings	24,000	1,12,000	Less: Depreciating	2,000	18,000
		1,49,000			1,49,000

Note: Drawings:
Cash – 10,000
Cheques – 14,000
24,000

Illustration 12: The following information is obtained from the books of Mr. Ranjan who maintained the same under single entry system.

(1) Receipts for the year ending 31-12-2011:

	₹
From debtors	1,76,250
Cash sales	41,250
Paid in by Ranjan	25,000

Payments made during the year

New plant bought	6,250
Drawings	15,000
Salaries	11,250
Wages	67,250
Interest paid	750
Rent paid	13,250
Light and power	4,750
Sundry expenses	21,250
Sundry creditors	76,250

Mr. Ranjan banks all the receipts and makes all payments by means of cheques.

(2) Assets and liabilities:

	1-1-2011	31-12-2011
	₹	₹
Sundry creditors	25,250	24,000
Sundry debtors	37,500	61,250
Bank balance	6,250	?
Stocks in trade	62,500	31,250
Plant	75,000	73,150

Prepare trading and profit and loss account and balance sheet.

(B.U. April 1992, 2nd Sem. B.Com June 2006)

S-12 Working Notes:

Before we prepare final a/c, we should identify missing items, and ascertain the same.

Missing items	*How to ascertain*
1. Credit sales	By preparing total debtors A/c
2. Credit purchase	By preparing total creditors A/c
3. Opening capital	By preparing opening statement & affairs
4. Bank balance at the end	By preparing bank A/c
5. Depreciation on plant	By comparing opg. & clg. Bal. of plant considering additions made during the year.

1. Credit Sales = ?

Total Debtors' A/c

Dr. Cr.

	(₹)		(₹)
To balance B/d	37,500	By cash A/c	1,76,250
To credit sales (Balancing figure)	2,00,000	By balance c/d	61,250
	2,37,500		2,37,500

2. Credit purchases: ?

Total Creditors A/c

Dr. Cr.

	(₹)		(₹)
To cash a/c	76,250	By Balance B/d	25,250
To balance c/d	24,000	By Credit purchases (Balancing figure)	75,000
	1,00,250		1,00,250

3. Opening Capital: ?

Opening statement of affairs as on 1.1.2011

Liabilities	₹	Assets	₹
Creditors A/c	25,250	Bank A/c	6,250
Capital (Balancing figure)	1,56,000	Debtors A/c	37,500
		Stock A/c	62,500
		Plant A/c	75,000
	1,81,250		1,81,250

4. Banks Balance at the end = ?

Bank Account

Dr. Cr.

	₹		₹
To Balance B/d 1.1.11	6,250	By new plant purchased	6,250
To debtors	1,76,250	By drawings	15,000
To cash sales	41,250	To salaries	11,250
To (Ranjan's) capital	25,000	To wages	67,250
		To interest	750
		To rent	13,250
		To light and power	4,750
		To sundry expenses	21,250
		To sundry creditors	76,250
		To balance c/d 31.12.11 (Balancing figure)	32,750
	2,48,750		2,48,750

5. Depreciation on plant: ?

	₹
Plant on 1.1.2011.............	75,000
+ Additions made during the year	6,250
	81,250
Less: plant on 31-12-2011	73,150
Depreciation	8,100

Trading and profit and loss A/c
For the year ended 31st Dec, 2011

Dr. Cr.

Particulars	₹	Particulars		₹
To opening stocks	62,500	By sales:		
To purchases (Credit)	75,000	Cash	41,250	
To wages	67,250	Credit	2,00,000	2,41,250
To gross profit c/d	67,750	By closing stock		31,250
	2,72,500			2,72,500
To salaries	11,250	By Gross profit		67,750
To interest	750			
To rent	13,250			
To light & power	4,750			
To sundry expenses	21,250			
To depreciation (as calculated)	8,100			
To net profit c/d	8,400			
	67,750			67,750

Balance sheet
as on 31st Dec, 2011

Liabilities		₹	Assets		₹
Creditors		24,000	Bank		32,750
	₹				
Opg. Capital	1,56,000		Debtors		61,250
+ Net profit	8,400		Stock		31,250
	1,64,400			₹	
(–) Drawings	15,000		Plants opg. bal.	75,000	
	1,49,400		+ Additions	6,250	

(Contd.)

(Contd.)

+ Additional capital introduced	25,000	1,74,400		81,250	
			(–) Depreciation	8,100	73,150
		1,98,400			1,98,400

Problem 13: You are given:

(a) The Balance sheet of Mr. A on 1-4-2011.

(b) The cash transactions for the year upto 31.3.2012

(c) A Summary of remaining transactions for the year upto 31.3.2012.

(a)

Liabilities	₹	Assets	₹
Bank overdraft	500	Cash in hand	70
Sundry creditors	3,600	Bills receivable	2,500
Bills payable	1,600	Sundry debtors	3,900
Capital	20,000	Stocks	7,530
		Plant and Machinery	4,700
		Land and Building	7,000
	25,700		25,700

	₹		₹
(b) To Balance B/d	70	By Balance (BOD) B/d	500
To debtors	29,000	By Salaries	4,900
To bills receivable	10,000	By Wages	1,580
To cash sales	3,700	By Bills payable	14,300
		By Sundry creditors	14,700
		By Office expenses	800
		By Drawings	4,500
		By Investment @ par 9% G.P. Notes on 1.10.11	1,000
		Balance on 31.3.12	
		Cash	40
		Bank	450
	42,770		42,770

(c) Credit sales	40,700
Discount to customers	200
Purchases	30,000
Discount received	100
B/R received	10,900
B/P issued	15,000
Stock 31.3.12	5,300

Provide for doubtful debts @ 5% on debtors outstanding.

Provide for depreciation on plant and machinery @ 5% and land and building @ 2½%.

Prepare trading and profit and loss account for the year ended 31st March, 2012 and balance sheet as on that date.

(CA Inter, May 1990, B.U. B.Com May 2001, Modified)

Solution: *Working Notes:*

Before we prepare trading and profit and loss account and balance sheet, we should identify the missing items given below and ascertain the same.

	Missing items	*How to ascertain*
1.	Debtors at the end	By preparing total debtors A/c
2.	B/R at the end	By preparing bills receivable A/c
3.	Creditors at the end	By preparing total creditors A/c
4.	Bills payable at the end	By preparing bills payable A/c

1. Debtors at the end = ?

Total Debtors' A/c

Dr. Cr.

	₹		₹
To balance B/d 1.4.11	3,900	By cash A/c	29,000
To credit sales	40,700	By bills receivable	10,900
		By discount allowed	200
		By balance c/d, 31.3.12 (Balancing figure)	4,500
	44,600		44,600

2. Bills receivable at the end = ?

Bills Receivable A/c

Dr. Cr.

	₹		₹
To balance B/d 1.4.11	2,500	By cash A/c	10,000
To debtors (B/R)	10,900	By balance c/d 31.3.12 (Balancing figure)	3,400
	13,400		13,400

3. Creditors at the end = ?

Total Creditors' A/c

Dr. Cr.

	₹		₹
To cash A/c	14,700	By balance B/d 1.4.11	3,600
To discount received	100	By credit purchases	30,000
To bills payable	15,000		
To balance c/d 31.3.12 (Balancing figure)	3,800		
	33,600		33,600

4. Bills payable at the end = ?

Bills Payable A/c

Dr. Cr.

	₹		₹
To cash A/c	14,300	By balance B/d 1.4.11	1,600
To balance c/d 31.3.12 (Balancing figure)	2,300	By creditors (B/P)	15,000
	16,600		16,600

Trading and Profit and Loss A/c

For the year ended 31st March, 2012

Dr. Cr.

Particulars	₹	Particulars		₹
To opening stocks 1.4.11	7,530	By sales:		
To purchases (as given)	30,000	cash	3,700	
To wages	1,580	credit	40,700	44,400
To gross profit c/d	10,590	To closing stock 31.3.12		5,300
	49,700			49,700
To salaries	4,900	By Gross profit B/d		10,590
To office expenses	800	To Discount received		100
To reserve for D. debts @ 5% on O/s debtors	225	To int. on GP Notes $\left(1000\times\frac{9}{100}\times\frac{6}{12}\right)$		45
To depreciation:-				
on land & building @ 2½%	175			
on plant and machinery @ 5%	235			
To discount allowed to customers	200			
To net profit c/d	4,200			
	10,735			10,735

Balance Sheet
as on 31st March, 2012

Capital and Liabilities		Amount ₹	Assets and Properties		Amount ₹
Sundry Creditors		3,800	Cash		40
Bills payable		2,300	Bills Receivable		3,400
	₹		Sundry Debtors	4500	
Opening Capital	20,000		Less: RDD	225	4,275
Add: N/P	4,200		Stocks		5,300
	24,200		Bank		450
Less: Drawings	4,500	19,700	Plant & Machinery	4,700	
			Less: Depreciation	235	4,465
			Land and Building	7,000	
			Less: Depreciation	175	6,825
			Investments – GP Notes –		1,000
			(Int. Due in G.P. Notes for 6 months		45
		25,800			25,800

Illustration 14: Mr. Prasad who has not kept complete set of books asks you to prepare his final accounts for the year ended 31-12-2011. You are however, able to obtain the following informatory:

Summary of Cash Book	₹	
Balance of cash 1.1.2011	5,170	
Receipts from debtors	42,050	
Payments to creditors	32,400	
Salaries	2,500	
Rent	1,200	
Electricity charges	360	
Printing and stationery	250	
Advertising	450	
Assets and liabilities:	31.12.10	31.12.11
	₹	₹
Sundry debtors	3,350	5,100
Sundry creditors	1,400	3,500
O/s advertising expense	NIL	250
Furniture	5,000	8,000
Machinery	8,000	8,000

The stocks on 31.12.2011 was valued at ₹ 4,500. But Mr. Prasad has no record of stock on 1-1-2011. However, he informs you that he invariably sells goods at cost plus 25% profit. He used goods worth ₹ 120 per month for personal use. 1/3 of rent and electricity charges to be treated as his personal expenses.

Depreciate furniture @ 5% and machinery @ 10%.

(B.U. Nov 1994 and 2nd Sem. B. Com. June, 2005)

Solution: *Working Notes:*

Before we prepare final accounts of Mr. Prasad, we should ascertain the hidden informality as given below:

Hidden information		How to ascertain By preparing:
1. Closing cash balance	-	Cash A/c
2. Credit sales	-	Total debtors A/c
3. Credit purchases	-	Total creditors A/c
4. Opening stocks	-	Memorandum trading A/c
5. Opening capital	-	Opening statement of affairs

1. Closing Cash Balance = ?

Cash Account

Dr. Cr.

	₹		₹
To Balance B/d (1.1.11)	5,170	By creditors	32,400
To Receipts from debtors	42,050	By salaries	2,500
		By rent	1,200
		By furniture	3,000
		By electricity charges	360
		By printing and stationery	250
		By advertising	150
		By balance c/d 31-12-11 (Balancing figure)	7,060
	47,220		47,220

2. Credit Sales = ?

Total Debtors' Account

Dr. Cr.

	₹		₹
To Balance B/d 1.1.11	3,350	By Cash A/c	42,050
To Credit Sales A/c (Balancing figure)	43,800	By Balance c/d 31-12-11	5,100
	47,150		47,150

3. Credit Purchases = ?

Total Creditor Account

Dr. Cr.

	₹		₹
To cash A/c	32,400	By balance B/d 1.1.11	1,400
To balance c/d 31.12.11	3,500	By credit purchases (Balancing figure)	34,500
	35,900		35,900

4. Opening Stock:

Memorandum Trading A/c (31-12-2012)

Dr. Cr.

To opening stock (1.1.11) (Balancing figure)		6,480	By Sales	43,800
To Purchases	34,500		To closing stocks	4,500
Less: Drawings goods	1,440	33,060		
To G/P $\left(42800\times\frac{25}{125}\right)$		8,760		
		48,300		48,300

5. Opening Capital:

Statement of Affairs as on 1-1-2011

Dr. Cr.

Liabilities	₹	Assets	₹
Sundry creditors	1,400	Stocks	6,480
Capital (Balancing figure)	26,600	Cash	5,170
		Debtors	3,350
		Furniture	5,000
		Machinery	8,000
	28,000		28,000

Note: Since Trading A/c is already prepared (i.e., 4), Let us prepare profit and loss A/c.

Profit and loss A/c
For the year ended 31st Dec, 2011

Dr. Cr.

Particulars		₹	Particulars	₹
To salaries		2,500	By gross profit B/d	8,760
To rent (1,200 x 2/3)		800		
To electricity charges (360 × 2/3)			240	
To printing & stationery		250		
To advertising	450			
Add: O/s advertising	250	700		
Depreciation:				
@ 5% on furniture		325		
@ 10% on machinery		800		
To Net Profit c/d		3,145		
		8,760		8,760

Note:- Drawings =

	₹
(1) Goods used for personal use @ 120 per month (120 x 12)	1,440
(2) Electricity charges – Personal expense (360 × 1/3)	120
(3) Rent – Personal = (1200 × 1/3)	400
Total drawings	1,960

Balance Sheet of Mr. Prasad
as on 31st December 2011

Liabilities		₹	Assets		₹
Sundry creditors		3,500	Cash		7,060
Advertising O/s		250	Sundry debtors	5,100	
Opg. capital	26,600		furniture	8,000	
+ Net profit	3,145		(5000 + 3000)		
	29,745		Less: depreciation	725	7,675
– Drawings	1,960	27,785	machinery	8,000	
			Less: Depreciation	800	7,200
			clg. stocks		4,500
		31,535			31,535

Note: Assumed that part of furniture i.e., ₹ 3,000 was purchased at the beginning of the accounting year and depreciation is changed on it accordingly.

Illustration 15: Raghupathi did not maintain his books of accounts properly. From the following data supplied to you. Prepare final accounts for the year ended 31-3-2012.

	₹
Opening stocks	10,000
Sundry creditors 1.4.2011	4,000
Cash on hand 1.4.2011	6,000
Furniture 1.4.2011	2,000
Salaries	6,800
Rent	2,400
Other expenses	4,800
Cash sales	8,000
Cash received from debtors	64,000
Cash paid to creditors	36,000
Cash purchases	4,000
Credit purchases	60,000
Closing stocks	8,000
Debtors on 31.3.2012	24,000
Drawings	8,000
Discount allowed to debtors	2,000
Donation given to Prime Minister's draught relief fund	2,000

He informs you that he invariably sells goods at a profit of $33^1/_3$% on cost. Ignore depreciations.

(B.U. April/May 1996)

Solution: *Working Notes:*

Let us dig out hidden information first and then proceed with the preparation of final accounts of Mr. Raghupathi.

Hidden informatory	*How to ascertain with the help of:*
(1) Total sales	G/p m cost $33^1/_3$% given.
(2) Credit sales	Total sales & cash sales
(3) Opening debtors	Total debtors A/c
(4) Closing creditors	Total creditors A/c
(5) Opening capital	Opening statement of affairs and
(6) Closing cash balance	Cash account

(1) Total sales = ?

To ascertain total sales, Raghupathi informs you that he sells his goods invariably at a profit of $33^1/_3$% on cost. Therefore, total sales can be ascertained as follows:

Cost of goods sold (Cost) = Opening stocks + purchases – closing stocks

= 10,000 – (4,000 + 60,000) – 8,000

$$= 66{,}000$$

$$\therefore \text{ Gross profit on cost } = \cancel{66{,}000}^{22{,}000} \times \frac{\cancel{33\text{-}1/3}^{1}}{\cancel{100}^{3}} = \frac{1}{3}$$

$$\therefore \text{ G/p } = ₹\ 22{,}000$$

Hence, total sales = Cost of goods sold + Gross profit

∴ ₹ 88,000 = 66,000 + 22,000

(2) Credit Sales : ?

Credit Sales = Total Sales – Cash Sales

∴ ₹ 80,000 = 88,000 – 8,000

(3) Opening Debtors = ?

Total Debtors A/c

Dr. Cr.

	₹		₹
To Balance B/d 1.4.11 (Balancing figure)	10,000	By Cash A/c	64,000
To Credit Sales	80,000	By Discount allowed	2,000
		By Balance c/d 31.3.12	24,000
	90,000		90,000

(4) Closing Creditors : ?

Total Creditors A/c

Dr. Cr.

	₹		₹
To Cash A/c	36,000	By Balance B/d 1.4.11	4,000
To Balance c/d 31-3-12 (Balancing figure)	28,000	By Credit purchases	60,000
	64,000		64,000

(5) Opening Capital:?

Statement of Affairs
as on 1st April 2011

Liabilities	₹	Assets	₹
Sundry creditors	4,000	Cash on hand	6,000
Capital (Balancing figure)	24,000	Furniture	2,000
		Sundry debtors	10,000
		Stocks	10,000
	28,000		28,000

(6) Closing Cash Balance = ?

Cash A/c

Dr. Cr.

	₹		₹
To Balance B/d 1.4.11	6,000	By salaries	6,800
To cash sales	8,000	By rent	2,400
To Receipts from debtors	64,000	By other expenses	4,800
		By sundry creditors	36,000
		By cash purchases	4,000
		By drawings	8,000
		By PM's draught fund	2,000
		By balance c/d 31.3.12 (Balancing figure)	14,000
	78,000		78,000

Trading and Profit and Loss A/c

For the year ended 31st March, 2012

Dr. Cr

Particulars		₹	Particulars		₹
To opening stocks 1.4.11		10,000	By sales:		
To Purchases:			Cash	8,000	
Cash	4,000		Credit	80,000	88,000
Credit	60,000	64,000	By closing stocks		8,000
By Gross profit c/d $\left(88000\times\frac{33\frac{1}{3}}{133\frac{1}{33}}\right)$		22,000			
		96,000			96,000
To Salaries		6,800	By Gross profit B/d		22,000
To Rent		2,400			
To other expenses		4,800			
To Discount allowed		2,000			
To Net Profit c/d		6,000			
		22,000			

Note: GP $33^1/_3$ On cost means of cost is ₹ 100 – G/P is $33^1/_3$
G/P on Sales means Sales = cost + GP. i.e. $(100 + 33^1/_3)$

$$\therefore G/P \text{ on Sales} = \frac{33\frac{1}{3}}{133\frac{1}{3}} \text{ or } \frac{1}{4} \text{ or } 25\%$$

Balance Sheet
as on 31st March, 2012

Liabilities			₹	Assets	₹
Sundry creditors			28,000	Cash	14,000
Opg. Capital		24,000		Stocks	8,000
Add: Net Profit		6,000		Sundry debtors	24,000
		30,000		Furniture	2,000
Less: Drawings:					
Cash	8,000				
Donation to PMs Fund	2,000	10,000	20,000		
			48,000		48,000

Illustration 16: Thomas does not maintain his books in the double entry system and bank account. From the following information prepare his profit and loss account and balance sheet as at June 30, 2012.

(A) Assets and Liabilities

	30.6.2011 ₹	30.6.2012 ₹
Stocks	19,800	1,13,200
Sundry creditors	31,000	14,500
Sundry debtors	1,18,000	1,25,000
Premises	90,000	90,000
Furniture	11,000	11,500
Air-conditioner	15,000	15,000

(B) Creditors as at 30.6.2011, includes ₹ 15,000 for purchase of air-conditioner.

(C) Cash transactions:

	₹
Cash as at 1.7.2011	15,000
Collections from debtors	1,60,800
Payments to Trade creditors	1,44,000
Rent, rates and taxes	11,500
Salaries	1,12,000
Sundry expenses	18,000
Sundry income	16,500
Drawing by Thomas	30,000
Loan from Mrs. Fernandis	23,000
Capital introduced	12,000
Cash sales	11,500
Cash purchases	15,000
Paid to creditors for air-conditioner	15,000

(D) Bad debts written-off ₹ 12,000

(J.C.W.A.)

Solution: To start with, let us identify the hidden information and ascertain the same as follows:

Hidden Information	*How to ascertain with the help of:*
(1) Closing cash balance	Bank A/c
(2) Credit sales	Total debtors A/c
(3) Credit purchases	Total creditors A/c
(4) Opening capital	Opening balance sheet

(1) Closing cash balance:?

Cash Account

Dr. Cr.

	₹		₹
To balance B/d 1.7.2011	15,000	By creditors (Trade)	1,44,000
To debtors	1,60,800	By rent, rates & taxes	11,500
To sundry income	16,500	By salaries	1,12,500
To capital introduced	12,000	By sundry expenses	18,000
To loan – Mrs. Fernandis	23,000	By drawings	30,000
To cash sales	11,500	By cash purchases	15,000
To balance c/d 30.6.2012	1,07,200	By creditors (air-conditioner)	15,000
(BOD – Balancing figure)		By furniture (11,500 – 11,000)	500
	3,46,000		3,46,000

(2) Credit Sales: ?

Total Debtors A/c

Dr. Cr.

	₹		₹
To balance B/d 30.6.11	1,18,000	By cash	1,60,800
To credit sales	1,69,000	By bad debts	1,200
(balancing figure)		By balance c/d 30.6.12	1,25,000
	2,87,000		2,87,000

(3) Credit Purchases: ?

Total Creditors A/c

Dr. Cr.

	₹		₹
To Cash	1,44,000	By Balance B/d 30.6.11	
		(31,000 – 15,000)	16,000
To Balance c/d 30.6.12	14,500	By Credit purchases	
		(Balancing figure)	1,42,500
	1,58,500		1,58,500

Note: Total creditors means total trade creditors – i.e. the persons to whom we owe money for purchase of goods. Non-trade creditors i.e., as for purchase of air-conditioner do not find place. Hence, opening balance of trade creditors = ₹ 31,000 – ₹ 15,000. Because it includes amount of creditors purchase of air conditioners.

(4) Opening Capital: ?

Opening Balance Sheet
as on 30th June, 2011

Liabilities	₹	Assets	₹
Creditors	31,000	Stocks	19,800
Capital (balancing figure)	2,37,800	Debtors	1,18,000
		Premises	90,000
		Furniture	11,000
		Air-conditioner	15,000
		Cash	15,000
	2,68,800		2,68,800

Trading and Profit and Loss A/c
for the year ended 30th June 2012

Dr. Cr.

Particulars		₹	Particulars		₹
To opening stocks 30.6.11		19,800	By Sales:		
To Purchases: Cash	15,000		Cash	11,500	
Credit	1,42,500	1,57,500	Credit	1,69,000	1,80,500
To Gross Profit c/d		1,16,400	To closing stocks		1,13,200
		2,93,700			2,93,700
To salaries		1,12,000	By gross profit B/d		1,16,400
To rent, rates and taxes		11,500	By sundry income		16,500
To sundry expenses		18,000	By net loss c/d		9,800
To bad debts		1,200			
		1,42,700			1,42,700

Balance Sheet
as on 30th June, 2012

Liabilities		₹	Assets	₹
	₹			
Opening capital	2,37,800		Premises	90,000
Add: additional capital	12,000		Furniture	11,500
	2,49,800		Air-coditioner	15,000

(Contd.)

(Contd.)

Less: Drawings	30,000		Sundry debtors	1,25,000
	2,19,800		Stocks	1,13,200
Less: Net loss incurred	9,800	2,10,000		
Sundry Creditors (Trade)		14,500		
Mrs. Fernandes loan		23,000		
Bank over draft		1,07,200		

Illustration 17: Mr. Prasad keeping his books under single entry system has placed the following facts before you :

(a) His statements of affairs as on 1-4-2011

(b) A summary of cash transactions for the year 2011-12

(c) A list of remaining transactions for the year 2011-12.

(a)

	₹			₹
Bank overdraft	37,500	Sundry debtors	1,12,500	
Creditors	75,000	Less: provision	5,625	1,06,875
Bills payable	4,500	Bills receivable		27,000
O/s General charges	3,000	Stocks on trade		1,05,000
Capital	2,28,000	Plant and machinery		75,000
		Premises		30,000
		Cash		4,125
	3,48,000			3,48,000

(b)

	₹		₹
To Balance B/d 1.4.11	4,125	By creditors	2,70,000
To bills receivable	75,000	By cash purchases	60,000
To receipts from debtors	3,27,000	By bills payable	1,20,000
To cash sales	61,500	By salaries	22,500
To Mrs. Prasad's loan	37,500	By rent and rates	13,500
		By general expenses	6,750
		By drawings	8,100
		By balance c/d 31.3.12	4,275
	5,05,125		5,05,125

(c)

	₹
Total sales	6,03,750
Total purchases	5,40,000
Discount allowed to debtors	1,500
B/R as at 31.3.2012	45,000
B/P accepted during the year	1,39,500
Stocks on 31.3.2012	1,27,500
Owing for O/s general charges	4,500
Bad debts	3,000
Prepaid rent	2,700
Discount allowed by creditors	3,000

Provide 5% for doubtful debts and 2½ % for discount on debtors. Depreciate premises by 2% and plant and machinery by 10%.

You are required to:

(a) Prepare trading and profit and loss account for the year ended 31st March, 2012 and

(b) Balance sheet of Mr. Prasad from the above details.

Solution: *Working Notes:*

Before preparing final a/c of Mr. Prasad, we have to list out missing items and know how to ascertain items as stated below:

	Missing Items	*How to ascertain by preparing:*
1.	B/R receivable received from debtors	B/R A/c
2.	Closing debtors balance	Total debtors A/c
3.	Closing bills payable	Bills payable A/c
4.	Closing creditors balance	Total creditors A/c

1. Bills receivable received from debtors: ?

Bills Receivable A/c

Dr. Cr.

	₹		₹
To balance B/d 1.4.11	27,000	By Cash	75,000
To debtors – B/R received (Balancing figure)	93,000	By Balance c/d 31.3.12	45,000
	1,20,000		1,20,000

2. Closing Balance of Debtors: ?

Total Debtors A/c

Dr. Cr.

	₹		₹
To balance B/d 1.4.11	1,12,500	By Cash	3,27,000
To credit sales	5,42,250	By bills receivable	93,000
		By bad debts	3,000
		By discount allowed	1,500
		By balance c/d 31.3.12 (Balancing figure)	2,30,250
	6,54,750		6,54,750

Note: Credit Sales = Total Sales – Cash sales

5,42,250 = 6,03,750 – 61,500

3. Closing Balance of Bills payable: ?

Bills Payable A/c

Dr. Cr.

	₹		₹
To cash A/c	1,20,000	By Balance B/d 1.4.11	4,500
To balance c/d 31.3.12	24,000	By Creditors (B/P issued)	1,39,500
(Balancing figure)			
	1,44,000		1,44,000

4. Closing Balance of Creditors: ?

Total Creditors A/c

Dr. Cr.

	₹		₹
To cash	2,70,000	By balance B/d 1.4.11	75,000
To bills payable	1,39,500	By credit purchases	4,80,000
To discount received	3,000		
To balance c/d 31.3.12			
(Balancing figure)	1,42,500		
	5,55,000		5,55,000

Note: Credit purchases = Total purchases – Cash purchases

∴ ₹ 4,80,000 = 5,40,000 – 60,000

Trading and Profit and Loss A/c

For the year ended 31st March, 2012

Dr. Cr.

Particulars		(₹)	Particulars		(₹)
To opening stocks 1.4.11		1,05,000	By Sales:		
To Purchases : Cash	60,000		Cash	61,500	
Credit	4,80,000	5,40,000	Credit	5,42,250	6,03,750
		86,250	By closing stocks 31.3.12		1,27,500
		7,31,250			7,31,250
To Salaries		22,500	By gross profit B/d		86,250
To Rent & rates	13,500		By discount received		3,000
Less: Prepaid rent	2,700	10,800			
To General expenses	6,750				
Add: O/s for 2011-12	4,500				
	11,250				
Less: O/s for 2010-11	3,000	8,250			

(Contd.)

(Contd.)

Less: R.D.D. @ 5% on Debtors	11,513			
Less: Old reserve	5,625	5,888		
To discount on debtors @ 2½%		5,467		
To discount allowed		1,500		
To depreciation on :-				
Premises @ 2%	600			
Plant & Machinery @ 10%	7,500	8,100		
To bad debts		3,000		
To net profit c/d		23,745		
		89,250		89,250

Note: Discount on Debtors : 2,30,250 – 11,513 = 2,18,677 × 2½/100
= 5,466.9 of 5,467

Balance Sheet
as on 31st March, 2012

Liabilities		₹	Assets		₹
Sundry creditors		1,42,500	Sundry debtors	2,30,250	
Bills payable		24,000	Less: RDD + Dis	16,980	2,13,270
Bank overdraft		37,500	Bills Receivable		45,000
O/s general expenses		4,500	Stocks		1,27,500
Mrs. Prasad's loan		37,500	Plant & Machinery	75,000	
Opening capital	2,28,000		Less: Depreciation	7,500	67,500
Add: Net profit	23,745		Premises	30,000	
	2,51,745		Less: Depreciation	600	29,400
Less: Drawings	8,100	2,43,645	Cash		4,275
			Prepaid expenses		2,700
	Total	4,89,645			4,89,645

Illustration 18: The books of Mr. Sudarshan showed the following figures.

Assets and Liabilities	31.3.2011	31.3.2012
	₹	₹
Cash in hand and at bank	3,400	19,950
Stocks-in-trade	20,000	25,000
Trade debtors	?	35,000
Trade creditors	?	18,500
Sundry assets	3,000	-

The cash book showed the following details:

	₹
Receipts from debtors	1,36,000
Private dividend paid in	2,000
Indirect expenses incurred	19,650
Drawings made during year	4,600
Payments to creditors	1,12,000
Discount allowed by them	1,200

Other details:

1. The cost of goods sold during the year 2011-12 ₹ 1,05,300
2. Mr. Sudarshan maintains a steady gross profit on sales @ 25%.
3. Bad debts written-off during the year ₹ 400 and past bad debts (already written-off) now recovered ₹ 200.

You are required to prepare:

(a) Trading and profit and loss account for the year ended 31st March, 2012

(b) Balance sheet of Mr. Sudarshan as on that date.

Solution: *Working Notes:*

To begin with, let us ascertain the missing items and then proceed with preparation of final accounts.

	Missing Items	*Ascertainment (How?) by Preparing:*
1.	Cash sales	Cash book
2.	Total sales	With the help of G/P rate given
3.	Credit sales	With the help of total sales and cash sales
4.	Opening debtors	By preparing total debtors A/c
5.	Credit purchases	With the help of accounting equations and
6.	Opening creditors	Preparing total creditors A/c
7.	Opening capital	Opening statement of affairs

1. Cash Sales = ?

Cash Book

Dr. Cr.

Receipts	₹	Payments	₹
To balance B/d 31.3.11	3,400	By indirect expenses	19,650
To debtors	1,36,000	By drawings	4,600
To additional capital (dividend)	2,000	By creditors	1,12,000
To bad debts recovered	200	By balance c/d 31.3.12	19,950
To cash sales (balancing figure)	14,600		
	1,56,200		1,56,200

2. Total sales made during year 2011-12 = ?

   Given cost of goods sold during the year ₹ 1,05,300 & G/P M Sales 25%.

   i.e., Cost of goods = Sales – G/P

   75 = 100 – 25

   If cost of goods 75 1,05,300

   100

   $$\frac{100}{75} \times 1,05,300 = 35100$$

   = 1,40,400

   Sales (Total) = 1,40,400

3. Credit sales = ?
   Credit sales = Total sales – Cash sales
   1,25,800 = 1,40,400 – 14,600

4. Opening Debtors = ?
5. Credit purchases: (Total purchases)
   Cost of goods sold = opening stock + purchases – closing stock
   ∴ Purchases = cost of goods sold + closing stock – opening stock
   = 1,05,300 + 25,000 – 20,000

Purchases (Total) ₹ 1,10,300

Note: It is assumed that purchases arrived at as ₹ 1,10,300 is credit purchases because no cash purchases are given in the problems.

6. Opening creditors = ?

Total Creditors A/c

Dr. Cr.

	₹		₹
To cash	1,12,000	By Balance B/d (Balancing figure) 31.3.11	21,400
To Discount received	1,200	By credit purchases	1,10,300
To Balance c/d 31.3.12	18,500		
	1,31,700		1,31,700

7. Opening capital =

Opening Statement of affairs
as on 31st March, 2011

Liabilities	₹	Assets	₹
Sundry creditors	21,400	Cash	3,400

(Contd.)

(Contd.)

Sundry capital (Balancing figure)	50,600	Stock-in-trade	20,000
		Sundry debtors	45,600
		Sundry assets	3,000
	72,000		72,000

Trading and Profit and Loss A/c
For the year ended 31st March, 2012

Dr. Cr.

Particulars	₹	Particulars		₹
To opening stock 31.3.11	20,000	By Sales:		
To purchases	1,10,300	Cash	14,600	
To gross Profit c/d	35,100	Credit	1,25,800	1,40,400
		By Closing Stock 31.3.12		25,000
	1,65,400			1,65,400
To indirect expenses	19,650	By gross profit B/d		35,100
To Bad debts	400	By discount received		1,200
To net profit c/d	16,450	By bad debts recovered		200
	36,500			36,500

Balance sheet
as on 31st March, 2012

Liabilities		₹	Assets	₹
Sundry creditors		18,500	Cash	19,950
Opening capital	50,600		Stock	25,000
Add: Net profit	16,450		Debtors	35,000
	67,050		Sundry assets	3,000
Less: Drawings	4,600	62,450		
Additional Capital (Dividend)		2,000		
		82,950		82,950

Total Debtors' A/c

Dr. Cr.

	₹		₹
To balance B/d 31.3.11 (Balancing figure)	45,600	By cash	1,36,000
To credit sales	1,25,800	By bad debts	400
		By balance c/d 31.3.12	35,000
	1,71,400		1,71,400

Problem 19: Mr. Nagan carries on business as a retail trader. He does not maintain his books under double entry system. Out of cash sales effected by him, he operates his business activities and retains always cash of ₹. 1,000 in hand and deposits the balance with bank.

The stock for the year ended 31st June, 2012 are lost. However, he informs you that he sells goods invariably at a profit of $33^1/_3$% on cost. From the following additional information supplied to you, you are asked to prepare his final accounts for the year ended 30th June, 2012.

Assets and Liabilities	1.7.2011 ₹	30.6.2012 ₹
Cash in hand	1,000	1,000
Sundry creditors	4,000	9,000
Cash at bank	9	8,000
Sundry debtors	10,000	35,000
Stock of goods	28,000	?

Analysis of his bank pass book leveals the following information:

	₹
Payment to creditors	70,000
Payment for business expenses	12,000
Receipt from debtors	75,000
Loan from Akash on 1.7.2011 @ 10% p.a.	10,000
Cash deposited into bank	10,000

Further, he paid ₹ 2,000 cash, to creditors for goods supplied and salaries ₹ 4000 in cash. He also withdraw cash for his personal expenses ₹ 8000.

(B.U. 2nd Sem. B.Com. June 2010 Modified)

Solution: *Working Notes:*

We have to ascertain the following items before we proceed with preparation of final accounts:

	Missing Items	How to ascertain
1.	Cash Sales	refer cash transactions
2.	Opening bank balance	refer pass book details
3.	Credit Sales	Prepare total debtors A/c
4.	Credit purchases	Prepare total creditors A/c
5)	Closing stock -	Prepare memorandum trading A/c or equation
6)	Opening capital -	Opening statement of affairs

(1) Cash Sales : ?

It is stated in the problem that Mr. Nagan operates business out of cash sales and deposits balance with bank ∴ Cash transactions effected should be referred as:

Cash A/c

Dr. Cr.

	₹		₹
To balance B/d 1.7.11	1,000	By creditors	2,000
To cash sales (Balancing figure)	24,000	By salaries	4,000
		By drawings	8,000
		By bank (Deposit)	10,000
		Balance c/d 30.6.12	1,000
	25,000		25,000

(2) Opening Bank Balance : ?

Bank Account

Dr. Cr.

	₹		₹
To debtors	75,000	By balance B/d	5,000
To Akash's loan	10,000	By creditors	70,000
To Cash A/c (Deposit)	10,000	By business expenses	12,000
		By balance c/d 30.6.12	8,000
	95,000		95,000

Here, bank A/c show a difference of ₹ 5,000 (cr) balance.
It is bank overdraft at beginning i.e., on 1.7.11.

(3) Credit Sales = ?

Total Debtors A/c

Dr. Cr.

	₹		₹
To balance B/d 1.7.11	10,000	By bank	75,000
To credit sales (Balancing figure)	1,00,000	By balance c/d 30.6.12	35,000
	1,10,000		1,10,000

(4) Credit Purchases :- ?

Total Creditors' A/c

Dr. Cr.

	₹		₹
To cash	2,000	By balance B/d 1.7.11	4,000
To bank	70,000	By credit purchases (Balancing figure)	77,000
To balance c/d 30.6.12	9,000		
	81,000		81,000

(5) Closing stock = ?

Given G/P is $33^1/_3$ on cost i.e. $\frac{33\text{-}\frac{1}{3}}{100}$ or $\frac{1}{3}$

∴ Gross profit on sales = $\frac{\text{Gross profit}}{\text{Sales}}$

Where sales = cost + gross profit

$100 + 33\text{-}^1/_3$

Sales = $133\text{-}^1/_3$

Gross profit on sales = Credit Sales + Cash Sales

1,00,000 + 24,000

$$G/P = ₹\ 31{,}000 = \cancel{1{,}24{,}000}^{31{,}000} \times \frac{\cancel{33\text{-}\frac{1}{3}}^{1}}{\cancel{133\text{-}\frac{1}{4}}_{4}}$$

Cost of goods sold = Sales / G/P

∴ 93,000 = 1,24,000 – 31,000

Closing stock = Opening stock + Purchases – Cost of goods sold

28,000 + 77,000 – 93,000

Closing Stock = ₹ 12,000

Alternatively

Memorandum Trading A/c

	₹			₹
To opening stock	28,000	By Sales:		
To purchases	77,000	Cash	24,000	
To gross profit	31,000	Credit	1,00,000	1,24,000
$\frac{33\text{-}\frac{1}{3}}{133\text{-}\frac{1}{3}} \times 1{,}24{,}000$		By closing stock (Balancing figure)		12,000
	1,36,000			1,36,000

(6) Opening Capital = ?

Opening Statement of Affairs (1.7.2011)

Liabilities	₹	Assets	₹
Creditors	4,000	Cash	1,000
Bank o/d Capital	5,000	Debtors	10,000
Opening capital		Stock	28,000
(Balancing figure)	30,000		
	39,000		39,000

Trading and Profit and Loss A/c
for the year ended 31st June 2012

Dr. Cr.

Particulars	₹	Particulars	₹
To opening stocks	28,000	By sales	1,24,000
To purchases (Credit)	77,000	By closing stock	12,000
To gross profit c/d	31,000		
	1,36,000		1,36,000
To business expenses	12,000	By gross profit B/d	31,000
To salaries	4,000		
To interest on loan 10,000 × 107	1,000		
To net profit c/d	14,000		
	31,000		31,000

Balance Sheet
as on 30th June 2012

Liabilities		Assets		
Sundry creditors		9,000	Cash in hand	1,000
Akash's Loan	10,000		Cash at bank	8,000
Add: O/s interest	1,000	11,000	Closing stock	12,000
Opening capital	30,000		Sy. Debtors	35,000
Add: Net profit	14,000			
	44,000			
Less: Drawings	8,000	36,000		
		56,000		56,000

Illustration 20: Sri Rama started his business on 1-1.2011, with a capital of ₹ 25,000. He bought furniture for ₹ 4,000. He borrowed ₹ 5,000 from his wife and introduced further capital of ₹ 3,000. He withdraws ₹ 600 every month. From the following information, prepare his trading and profit and loss account and balance sheet as on 31st December, 2011.

	₹
Sales (including cash sales ₹ 30,000)	1,00,000
Purchases (including cash purchases ₹ 10,000)	75,000
Carriage inwards	700
Wages paid	300
Discount allowed to Debtors	800
Salary paid	6,200
Bad debts written-off	1,500
Trade expenses	1,200
Advertisement expenses	2,200

Sri Rama used goods worth ₹ 1,300 for private purposes and paid ₹ 500 to his son which is not recorded. On 31-12-2011, his debtors were ₹ 21,000 and creditors ₹ 15,000. Stock in trade was valued at ₹ 10,000 on that date. Furniture is to be depreciated by 10% p.a.

(B.U. April 1992, Non-Sem. B.Com.)

Solution:

(1) In this problem, the following missing items are to be calculate:

	Missing items	How to calculate
1.	Cash received from Dehtors	Prepare total debtors a/c
2.	Cash paid to creditors	Prepare total creditors a/c
3.	Closing cash balance	Prepare cash a/c

(2) Since it is new business the question of: (a) opening stock, (b) opening debtors and (c) opening creditors does not arise in this problem.

Ascertainment of Missing Items

(1) Cash received from debtors

Total debtors a/c

Dr. Cr.

	(₹)		(₹)
To credit sales (1,00,000–30,000)	70,000	By cash (Bal. fig.)	46,700
		By bad debts	1,500
		By discount	800
		By balance c/d 30/12/11	21,000
	70,000		70,000

(2) Cash paid from creditors = ?

Total creditors a/c

Dr. Cr.

	(₹)		(₹)
To cash paid (Bal-fig)	50,000	By credit purchases	65,000
To balance c/d 31.12.12	15,000	(75,000 – 10,000)	
	65,000		65,000

(3) Closing balance cash = ?

Cash Account

Dr. Cr.

	(₹)		(₹)
To capital (1.1.11)	25,000	By furniture 1.1.11	4,000
To wife's loan	5,000	By drawings (600 × 12)	7,200
To further capital	3,000	By cash purchase	10,000
To cash sales	30,000	By carriage inwards	700
To Debtors	46,700	By wages	300
		By salaries	6,200
		By trade expenses	1,200
		By advertisement	2,200
		By drawings (son)	500
		By Creditors	50,000
		By balance c/d 31.12.11	27,400
	1,09,000		1,09,700

Trading and Profit and Loss A/c
for the year ended 31st Dec, 2011

Dr. Cr.

Particulars	₹	Particulars	₹
To purchases 75,000		By sales	1,00,000
Less: Personal use-goods 1,300	73,700	By closing stock	10,000
To wages	300		
To carriage inwards	700		
To gross profit c/d-	35,300		
	1,10,000		1,10,000
To salaries	6,200	By gross profit B/d	35,300
To discount allowed	800		
To bad debts	1,500		

(Contd.)

(Contd.)

To trade expenses To advertisement To depreciation @ 10% on Furniture To Net profit c/d	1,200 2,200 400 23,000		35,300
	35,300		

Balance Sheet of Sri Rama
as on 31st December, 2011

Liabilities		₹	Assets		₹
Sundry creditors		15,000	Cash balance		27,400
Wife's loan		5,000	Stock		10,000
Opening capital	25,000		Sundry debtors		21,000
+ Further capital	3,000		Furniture	4,000	
	28,000		Less: Depreciation	400	3,600
Less: Drawings	9,000				
	19,000				
+ Net profit	23,000	42,000			
		62,000			62,000

Illustration 21: Mr. Niranjah furnishes you the following information:

Assets and liabilities	1.4.11	31.3.12
	₹	₹
Cash	1,500	6,000
Bank	13,500	?
Debtors	37,500	?
Stock	1,72,500	?
Fixed assets	52,500	?
Prepaid expenses	7,500	11,250
Outstanding expenses	6,000	6,750
Creditors	?	30,000
Loan from Ashok	?	22,500

Further, during the year :

(a) Mr. Niranjan collected ₹ 6,00,000 from customers and paid ₹ 2,62,500 to suppliers all through the bank.

(b) Credit purchases ₹ 3,22,500
Returns outwards ₹ 60,000

Credit Sales ₹ 6,75,000
Returns inwards ₹ 45,000

(c) Payments for expenses ₹ 1,95,000 out of which ₹ 45,000 were paid in cash.
(d) ₹ 1,05,000 withdrawn from the bank out of which ₹ 37,500 were used for personal expenses.
(e) Mr. Ashok was paid in cash:
Loan instalment ₹ 15,000
Interest on loan ₹ 3,000
(f) Gross profit margin – 50% on sales
(g) Depreciation on fixed assets @ 20%.

You are required to prepare final accounts of Mr. Niranjan for the year ended 31st March, 2012.

Solution: *Working Notes:*

In this problem, the missing items are clearly stated. Therefore, we have to find out missing items as stated below:

	Missing items	*How to ascertain*
1.	Cash confirmation	Prepare cash A/c
2.	Closing balance of bank	Prepare bank A/c
3.	Closing balance of debtors	Total debtors A/c
4.	Closing stock	With the help of accounting equation.
5.	Fixed assets (closing)	No change in value unless additions are made during the year.
6.	Opening creditors	Total creditors A/c
7.	Loan from ashok (opening balance)	With the help of loan repaid and loan O/s
8.	Opening capital	Opening statement of affairs

9. Treatment of prepaid and O/s expenses:
(a) Prepaid expenses: Add: Prepaid expenses of last year to the expenses paid during the year.
Deduct: Expenses prepaid during the current year (i.e., closing balance) from expenses paid during the year and again show them as an asset in balance sheet under current assets.
(b) Outstanding expenses: Add: Expenses outstanding at the end of the year to be expenses paid during the year and again show the same liability in the balance sheet under current liabilities.
Deduct: Expenses outstanding last year from the expenses paid during the current year.

(1) Confirmation of cash balance given in the problem:

Cash Account

Dr. Cr.

	₹		₹
To Balance B/d 1.4.11	1,500	By expenses	45,000
To Bank (Withdrawal)	67,500	By Ashok's loan repaid	15,000
		By interest on loan	3,000
		By balance c/d 31.3.12	6,000
	69,000		69,000

Note: Withdraw from Bank:	₹
Total amount withdrawn	1,05,000
Less: used for personal expenses	37,500
∴ Drawn for business purpose	67,500

(2) Closing Balance of cash:

Bank Account

Dr. Cr.

	₹		₹
To balance B/d 1.4.11	13,500	By creditors	2,62,500
To debtors	6,00,000	By expenses paid (1,95,000 – 45,000)	1,50,000
		By cash A/c- office me	67,500
		By drawings	37,500
		By balance c/d 31.3.12 (Balancing figure)	96,000
	6,13,500		6,13,500

(3) Closing Balance of Debtors:

Total Debtors A/c

Dr. Cr.

	₹		₹
To balance B/d 1.4.11	37,500	By bank	6,00,000
To credit sales	6,75,000	By returns inwards	45,000
		By balance c/d 31.3.12 (Balancing figure)	67,500
	7,12,500		7,12,500

(4) Closing Stock: Given G/P on sales = 50%, Sales (credit) ₹ 6,75,000 and returns inwards ₹ 45,000.

$\therefore$ Gross profit $= \frac{50}{100} \times$ Net sales i.e., $(6,75,000 - 45,000) \times \frac{50}{100}$

(i) $= \therefore$ Gross profit = 3,15,000

(ii) Cost of goods sold = Net sales – Gross profit

$\therefore$ ₹ 3,15,000 = 6,30,000 – 3,15,000

(iii) Closing Stock = Opening stock + purchases – cost of goods sold

₹ 1,20,000 = 1,72,500 + (3,22,500 – 60,000) – 3,25,000

Closing stock = ₹ 1,20,000

(5) Fixed Assets: (closing balance)

Unless additions are made during the year, there cannot be change in the value of fixed assets. Therefore, closing balance of fixed assets are ₹ 52,500/- only.

(6) Opening Creditors:

Total Creditors A/c

Dr. Cr.

	₹		₹
To bank	2,62,500	By balance B/d (Balancing figure) 1.4.11	30,000
To returns outwards	60,000	By credit purchases	3,22,500
To balance c/d 31.3.12	30,000		
	3,52,500		3,52,500

(7) Loan from Ashok (Opening balance)

	₹
Loan repaid during the year	15,000
Add: O/s loan on 31.3.12	22,500
Loan at beginning	37,500

(8) Opening capital:

Opening statement of Affairs
as on 1st April, 2011

Liabilities	₹	Assets	₹
O/s expenses	6,000	Bank	13,500
Creditors	30,000	Cash	1,500
Ashok's loan	37,500	Debtors	37,500
Capital (Balancing figure)	2,11,500	Stock	1,72,500
		Fixed assets	52,500
		Prepaid expenses	7,500
	2,85,000		2,85,000

Trading and Profit and Loss A/c
for the year ended 31st March, 2012

Dr. Cr.

Particulars	₹	Particulars	₹
To opening stocks 1.4.11	1,72,500	By Sales 6,75,000	
To Purchases 3,22,500		Less: Returns 45,000	6,30,000
Less: Returns 60,000	2,62,500	Closing stock	1,20,000
			7,50,000
To Gross profit c/d	3,15,000	By Gross profit B/d	3,15,000
	7,50,000		
₹			
To expenses paid 1,95,000			
Add: Prepaid expenses 1.4.11 7,500			
2,02,500			
Less: Prepaid expenses 31.3.12 11,250			
1,91,250			
Add: O/s expenses 31.3.12 6,750			
1,98,000			
Less: O/s expenses 1.4.11 6,000	1,92,000		
To interest on loan	3,000		
To depreciation on fixed assets	10,500		
To net profit c/d	1,09,500		
	3,15,000		3,15,000

Balance sheet of Mr. Niranjan
as on 31st March, 2012

Liabilities	₹	Assets	₹
₹			
Opening Capital 2,11,500		Fixed assets 52,500	
Add: Net profit 1,09,500		Less: Depreciation 10,500	42,500
3,21,000		Cash	6,000
Less: Drawings 37,500	2,83,500	Bank	96,000
Creditors	30,000	Debtors	67,500
Loan from Ashok	22,500	Stock	1,20,000
Outstanding expenses	6,750	Prepaid expenses	11,250
	3,42,750		3,42,750

QUESTIONS

Section A

1. What do you mean by single entry system?
2. State any two drawbacks of single entry system.
3. Mention two merits of single entry system.
4. Distinguish between statement of affairs and balance sheet. Any 2
5. Mention different types of single entry system.
6. What is pure single entry system?
7. What is single entry system?
8. What is quasi single entry system?
9. Given the specimen of B/R A/c.

Section B

1. "Single entry system is incomplete, inaccurate, unscientific and unsystematic method of recording transactions". Discuss with four reasons.
2. Ascertain purchases when cost of goods sold is ₹ 2,00,000, opening stock ₹ 20,000 and closing stock ₹ 50,000.

   (B.U. 2nd Sem. June 2005)

   Ans.: Purchases ₹ 2,30,000
3. Ascertain sales when: cost of goods sold is ₹ 80,000 and percentage of gross profit on sales 20%.

   (B.U. 2nd Sem. June 2005)

   Ans.: ₹ 1,00,000
4. From the following particulars of Mr. Ananth who keeps his books under single entry systems, ascertain total sales.

   Opening stock ₹ 36,000; closing stock ₹ 45,000,
   Purchases ₹ 1,80,000 and wages ₹ 21,000.
   Rate of gross profit on sales = $33^{1}/_{3}$%.
   Ans.: Sales = ₹ 2,88,000

   (B.U. 2nd Sem. June 2005)
5. Ascertain opening stock when: Purchases ₹ 1,20,000, wages ₹ 40,000, Sales ₹ 2,00,000, Closing stock ₹ 30,000 and G/P m sales 25%.

   B.U. 2nd Sem. June 2006

   Ans.: Opening stock ₹ 20,000
6. From the following information, calculate total sales.

	₹		₹
Opening balance of debtors	30,800	Returns outwards	8,700
B/R at the beginning	7,800	B/R dishonoured	1,800
B/R encashed during the year	20,900	B/R at end of the year	6,000
Cash received from debtors	70,000	Debtors at end of the year	25,500
Bad debts written-off	2,800	Cash Sales as per CD	40,900.

(B.U. 2nd Sem. B.Com. June 2006)

Ans.: ₹ 1,36200

7. Prepare total debtors A/c and B/R A/c for the year ending 31.3.2012 from the following:

	₹
Total sales	1,12,500
Cash sales	29,450
Returns inwards	450
Discount allowed	150
Cash received from debtors	69,400
Cash received against B/R	2,900
Debtors on 1.4.11	39,250
Debtors on 31.3.12	49,850
B/R on 1.4.11	1,900
B/R on 31.3.12	1,450

(BU. 2nd Sem. B.Com. June 2007)

8. Mention any five features of SES.

(B.U 2nd Sem. B. Com. June 2007)

9. Briefly explain stages in converting single entry systems into double entry system.

(BU. 2nd Sem. B. Com. June 2007)

10. Give any five difference between single-entry system and double-entry system.
11. Distinguish between statement of affairs and balance sheet.
12. What are the steps involved in conversism or single-entry into double entry.
13. What are the objectives of converting single-entry into double-entry?
14. State any 5 drawbacks of single entry system.
15. "An accounting system without double entry principle is incomplete" Why? give your reason.
16. Distinguish between the percentage of gross profit on sales and on cost.

UNIT – III

Hire Purchase System

3.1 Introduction
3.2 Meaning of hire purchase system (H.P.S.) and instalment system
3.3 Distinction between hire purchase and instalment system
3.4 Definition of hire purchase system
3.5 Hire purchase agreement – contents
3.6 Important terms used under H.P.S.
3.7 Calculation of interest : Problems and solutions
3.8 Accounting procedure:
  (a) In the books of hire purchaser
  (b) In the books of hire vendor
3.9 Problems and solutions
3.10 Default and Repossession
  (a) Partial repossession
  (b) Complete / full repossession

3.1 INTRODUCTION

Purchase of goods, may be cash purchases or credit purchases.

Cash purchases is a case where the price of the goods purchased is paid in one lumpsum, immediately.

Credit purchases is a case where the price of the goods purchased will be paid after the expiry of the stipulated period. In other words, under credit purchase, the payment of price of the goods purchased is postponed or deferred to a future date. Such a credit purchase is further classified as:

(a) Hire purchase system
(b) Instalment purchase system

3.2 MEANING OF HIRE PURCHASE AND INSTALMENT PURCHASE SYSTEM

Hire purchase system:

Hire purchase system is one under which goods are purchased or sold with certain stipulations. Such stipulations are:

(i) That the buyer acquires the possession of goods (i.e., delivery) immediately on signing the agreement.

(ii) That the ownership of goods is transferred from the hire vendor to the hire purchaser only on the payment of the last instalment.

(iii) That the purchase price of goods is paid in certain number of instalments.

(iv) That the buyer can make use of the goods till payment of the last instalment

(v) That the vendor continues to be the owner of the goods till the payment of the last instalment.

(vi) That the hire purchaser should keep the goods in good condition till the payment of the last instalment.

(vii) That the hire purchaser has a right to terminate the contract at any time.

(viii) That hire vendor can take back the possession of goods in case if the hire purchaser makes default in payment of any instalment.

Thus, hire purchase is a contract under which a person called hire purchaser takes the possession of goods immediately on signing the agreement and agrees to pay the price of the goods in certain number of instalments.

Instalment Purchase System

Instalment purchase is also a credit purchase system where:

(i) Full price of the goods is not paid by the buyer to the seller at once.

(ii) The ownership in goods is passed on from seller to the buyer immediately on signing the agreement itself. Hence, the buyer becomes the owner of goods immediately as in case of sale.

(iii) The purchase price of goods is paid in certain number of instalments.

(iv) The seller has no right to take back the goods for default in payment of any instalment.

(v) The buyer can resell the goods to the third party even before paying the last instalemnt, where the third party gets better title of goods.

3.3 DISTINCTION BETWEEN HIRE PURCHASE SYSTEM AND INSTALMENT PURCHASE SYSTEM

Points of difference	Hire purchase system	Instalment purchase system
1. Nature of contract	Is an agreement of hiring	Is an agreement of sale.
2. Transfer of property or ownership of goods	Ownership in goods remains with the seller till the payment of the last instament	Onwership of goods passes from seller to the buyer immediately on signing the agreement itself.

(Contd.)

(Contd.)

3. Repossess on of goods	Seller can repossess the goods for default in payment of any instalment by the buyer.	Seller cannot repossess the goods for non-payent of any instalment, but can sue the buyer in the court of law for default in payment.
4. Governance	Is governed by hire purchase act, (statue) 1972	Is not governed by any such act or statue.
5. Right of disposal	Buyer cannot sell, destroy, damage, transfer or pledge the goods.	Buyer can do all such things because he has already become the owner of goods.
6. Return of goods	Buyer can return the goods if he doesn't want to pay remaining instalments.	Goods cannot be returned by the buyer unless there is some default on the part of seller.
7. Repair of goods	As the seller continues to be the owner of goods till the payment of last instalment, it is his responsibility to get the goods repaired normally	As the buyer becomes the owner of goods on signing the agreement itself, seller is not at all responsible to get the goods repaired.
8. Forfeiture of instalments paid	In the event of default in payment of any instalment, the vendor can forfeit all the money paid by the buyer so far.	In the event of default money paid till the date of default should be treated as payment towards the part of selling price.

3.4 HIRE PURCHASE SYSTEM – DEFINITION

Andrew Munro defines hire purchase as:

> "In case of hire purchase agreements, the property in goods does not pass to the buyer until all the instalments have been paid. Each hire purchase instalment represents a payment on account of cash value of goods plus interest on outstanding balance of the cash value. If, however, he defaults, then, in most cases, the seller has power to recover the goods and total amount which has been paid by the hire purchaser represents the cost of hire purchaser's use."

Statutory Definiton – Hire Purchase Act, 1972, which is applicable to whole India except Jammu and Kashmir, which has come into effect from 1st September, 1973 defines:

(1) Hire Purchase Agreement [Section 2(c)]

"Hire purchase agreement means an agreement under which goods are lent on hire and under which the hirer has an option to purchase them in accordance with the terms of agreement and includes an agreement under which:

(i) Possession of goods is delivered by the owner thereof to a person on condition that such person pays the agreed amount in periodical instalments:

(ii) The property in goods is to pass to such a person on the payment of last instalment and

(iii) Such a person has the right to terminate the agreement at any time before the property so passes."

3.5 IMPORTANT TERMS USED UNDER HIRE PURCHASE SYSTEM

(2) Hire Purchase Price [Section 2(d)]

Hire purchase price means the total sum payable by the hirer under a hire purchase agreement in order to complete the purchase of or acquisition of property in goods to which the agreement relates and includes any sum so payable by the hirer under the hire purchase agreement by way of deposit or other initial payment.

(3) Hirer [Section 2(e)]

A hirer means a person who obtains or has obtained the possession of the goods from an owner under a hire purchase agreement.

(4) Cash Price [Section 4(1)(b)]

Cash price means the price at which the goods may be purchased by the hirer for cash.

(5) Hire purchase charges [Section 9(2)]

Hire purchase charges mean the difference between the hire purchase price and cash price as stated in the hire purchase agreement.

(6) Net Cash Price [Section 8(1)(e)]

Net cash price means the cash price of the goods sold on hire purchase less any deposit, payable by the hirer by way of initial payment.

(7) Net Hire Purchase Price: [Section 8(1)(e)]

Net hire purchase price means the total amount of hire purchase price of goods sold under hire purchase. The following amounts, if included in the hire purchase price, shall be deducted to determine the net hire purchase price:

(i) amount payable to cover the expenses of delivering the goods to the order of hirer.

(ii) amount payable to cover registration or other fees in respect of goods sold on hire purchase.

(iii) amount payable for insurance in respect of the hire purchase goods.

(8) Net Hire Purchase Charges [Section 8(1)(d)]

Net hire purchase charges in respect of goods sold on hire purchase means the difference between net hire purchase price and net cash price of such goods.

(9) Cash Price Instalment: [Section 7(1)(a)]

Cash price instalment in relation to hire purchase instalment means the amount which bears to the net cash price, the same proportion, as the hire purchase instalment bears to the total amount of hire purchase price.

As such, the formula for determining the cash price instalment can be put as follows:

$$\frac{\text{Hire purchase instalment}}{\text{Hire purchase price}} \times \text{Net cash price}$$

Form and Contents of Hire Purchase Agreement (Sections 3 and 4)

Every hire purchase agreement must be in writing and should be signed by the parties thereof. It should state the following:

(a) The hire purchase price of goods to which the agreement relates.

(b) Cash price of such goods.

(c) The date on which the agreement shall be deemed to have commenced.

(d) The number of instalments in which the hire purchase price is to be paid and the amount of each of those instalments, and the date or mode of determining the date upon which it is payable and the person to whom and the place where it is payable.

(e) The goods to which the agreement relates in a manner sufficient to identify them.

3.6 CALCULATION OF INTEREST

Based on the information available in the problem, different techniques have to be adopted for calculation of interest. Accordingly, there are five types of problems:

1. When the rate of interest, cash price, amount of instalment and number of instalments are given.
2. When the rate of interest and instalments are given and total cash price is not given.
3. When the instalments are given exclusive of interest.
4. When the total cash price and instalments are given but rate of interest is not given.
5. When cash price is not given, but reference to annuity table, rate of interest. and instalments are given in the problem.

I. When the rate of interest, cash price, amount of instalments and number of instalments are given in the problem.

Illustration 1

Prasad purchased a motor car on hire purchase system from Tata Motors on 1.1.2010. The cash price of motor car is ₹ 84,000. ₹ 22,500 is paid on signing the agreement and balance is to be paid in three equal annual instalments of ₹ 22,500. The rate of interest is 50% per annum.

Calculate the amount of interest included in each instalment.

Solution

Calculating on interest included in each instalment

Date	Details of calculation	Amount ₹
1.1.2010	Cash price of motor car	84,000
1.1.2010	Less: Cash down paid	22,500
1.1.2010	Outstanding balance	61,500
31.12.10	Add: Interest for the year 2010 $\left(61,500 \times \frac{5}{100}\right)$	3,075
		64,575
31.12.10	Less: I instalment	22,500
1.1.11	Outstanding balance	42,075
31.12.11	Add: Interest for the year 2011 $\left(42,075 \times \frac{5}{100}\right)$	2,104
		44,179
31.12.11	Less: II instalment	22,500
1.1.12	Outstanding balance	21,679
31.12.12	Add: Interest for the year 2012 (i.e., instalment – O/s balance (22,500 – 21,679)	821
	Outstanding balance	22,500
31.12.12	Less: Last instalment	22,500
		– 0 –

Illustration 2

On 1st Jan, 2009, a machinery was purchased on hire purchase system. The payment is to be made as follows:

₹ 4,000 on signing the agreement and ₹ 4,000 annually for next 3 years. The cash price of the machine is ₹ 14,900, and rate of interest is 50% p.a. Calculate the total interest payable and interest included in each instalment.

Solution 2

A. Total interest payable = Hire purchase price – cash price

∴ ₹ 1,100 = 16,000 – 14,900

(i) Hire purchase price = Down payment + Total amount of instalments

= 4,000 + 4,000 × 3

= ₹ 16,000

B. Calculation of interest included in each instalment:

Date	Details of calculation	Amount ₹
1.1.2009	Cash price of machinery	14,900
1.1.2009	Less: Cash down payment made	4,000
1.1.2009	Outstanding Balance	10,900
31.12.2009	Add : Interest for the year 2009	545
	$\left(10900 \times \frac{5}{100}\right)$	11,445
31.12.2009	Less: I instalment paid	4,000
1.1.2010	Outstanding Balance	7,445
31.12.2010	Add: Interest for the year 2010	372
	$\left(7.445 \times \frac{5}{100}\right)$	7,817
31.12.2010	Less: II instalment paid	4,000
1.1.2011	Outstanding balance	3,817
31.12.2011	Add: Interest for the year 2011 (i.e., instalment – O/s balance) 4,000 – 3,817	183
		4,000
31-12-2011	Less: Last instalment	4,000
		– 0 –

II: Calculation of cash price – Work back Method: i.e., when the rate of interest and instalments are given but total cash price is not given.

In case if the cash price of an asset purchased is not given in the problem, it is necessary to ascertain it because asset account cannot be capitalised at a price which is more than the cash price.

Procedure for calculation of cash price

To start with, take last instalment, say third instalment, calculate the interest adopting formula $\frac{\text{rate}}{100+\text{rate}}$ (e.g. $\frac{5}{105}$) instalment, deduct such interest from third instalment, to the balance available add amount of second instalment (as per our example), calculate interest on the total (i.e., last instalment – interest + 2nd instalment) adopting the same formula i.e., $\frac{5}{105}$ deduct again the interest from the total given above, add amount of I instalment to the balance, and now calculate interest on the total [i.e., (last instalment – interest + second instalment) – interest for second instalment + first instalment amount) adopting formula $\frac{5}{105}$ and deduct interest from that total and now add cash down paid to be balance the sum total is said to be cash price of an asset.

Let us discuss the procedure with concrete.

Examples:

(a) When instalments are uniform:

Illustration 3

Calculate the cash price of the machine from the following information:

	₹
(1) Down payment made on 1.1.2009	10,000
(2) Balance in four equal annual instalments at end of each year	10,000
(3) Hire purchase price	50,000
(4) Rate of interest – 5% p.a.	

Solution

Date	Details of calculation	Amount ₹
31.12.12	4th or last instalment due	10,000
	Less: interest $10,000\times\frac{5}{105}$	476
01.01.12	O/s Balance	9,524
	Add: third instalment	10,000
		19,524

(Contd.)

(Contd.)

	Less: Interest $19{,}524 \times \frac{5}{105}$	930
1.1.11	O/s Balance	18,594
	Add: 2nd Instalment	10,000
		28,594
	Less: Interest $28{,}594 \times \frac{5}{105}$	1,361
1.1.10	O/s Balance	27,233
	Add: 1st instalment	10,000
		37,233
	Less: Interest $10{,}000 \times \frac{5}{105}$	1,773
1.1.09	O/s Balance	35,460
1.1.09	Add: Cash down paid	10,000
1.1.09	Cash price	45,460

B. Calculation of cash price when the instalments are not uniform

Illustration 4

Calculate the cash price of an asset from the following:-

(1) ₹ 3,000 is paid at the time of agreement.

(2) ₹ 21,600, ₹ 20,700, ₹ 19,800 and ₹ 18,900 at the end if 1st, 2nd, 3rd and 4th year respectively as intalments.

(3) Rate of interest is 5% p.a.

(B.U. (Non-semester Scheme) B.Com. April 2001)

Solution: Calculation of cash price

Date	Working details	Amount ₹
End of 4h year	Last instalment due	18,900
	Less: interest $18{,}900 \times \frac{5}{105}$	900
Beg. of 4th year	O/s Balance	18,000

(Contd.)

(Contd.)

	Add: 3rd instalment	19,800
		37,800
	Less: interest $37,800 \times \frac{5}{105}$	1800
@ beg of III year	O/s Balance	36,000
	Add: 2nd instalment	20,700
		56,700
	Less: Interest $56,700 \times \frac{5}{105}$	2,700
@ beg of II year	O/s Balance	54,000
	Add: Ist instalment	21600
Beg. Of I year	Cash price	75,600
	Less: Interest $75,600 \times \frac{5}{105}$	3,600
	O/s Balance	72,000
	Add cash	3,000
	Cash	75,000

Illustration 5

Calculate cash price of an asset:

Down payment ₹ 1,500, first instalment ₹ 10,800, second instalment ₹ 10,350, third instalment ₹ 9,900 and fourth instalment ₹ 9,450. Payable at the end of each year. Rate of interest is 5% p.a.

(B.U. (Non-semester B.Com) Nov. 2000)

Calculation of cash price:

Date	Working Details	Amount ₹
End of 4th year	Last instalment due	9,450
	Less: Interest $9,450 \times \frac{5}{105}$	450
Beg. of 4th year	O/s Balance	9,000
	Add: 3rd instalment	9,900
		18,900
	Less: Interest $18,900 \times \frac{5}{105}$	900

(Contd.)

(Contd.)

Beg of 3rd year	O/s Balance Add: 2nd instalment	18,000 10,350
		28,350
	Less: Interest $28,350 \times \frac{5}{105}$	1,350
Beg of 2nd year	O/s Balance Add: Ist instalment	27,000 10,800
		37,800
	Less: Interst $37,800 \times \frac{5}{105}$	1,800
Beg of 1st year Beg of 1st year	O/s Balance Add: Cash down paid	36,000 1,500
Beg. of 1st year	Cash price	37,500

Illustration 6

Ms. Nidhi purchases a motor car on hire purchase system. Calculate the cash price of the motor car from the following:

Down payment = ₹ 20,000; 1st yearly instalment = ₹ 28,000; 2nd yearly instalment = ₹ 36,000; 3rd yearly instalment = ₹ 33,000; Rate of interest 10% p.a.

(B.U. (Semester scheme) B.Com. Dec., 2006)

Solution:

Calculation of cash price

Date	Working details	Amount ₹
End of 3rd year	Last instalment due Less: Interest $33,000 \times \frac{10}{110}$	33,000 3,000
Beg. of 3rd year	O/s Balance Add: 2nd instalment	30,000 36,000
		66,000
	Less: Interest $66,000 \times \frac{10}{110}$	6,000

(Contd.)

(Contd.)

Beg of II year	O/s Balance Add: 1st instalment	60,000 28,000
		88,000
	Less: Interest $88,000 \times \frac{10}{110}$	8,000
Beg of I year Beg of I year	O/s Balance Add: Cash down paid	80,000 20,000
Beg. of I year	Cash price	1,00,000

C. When quarterely instalments are given:

Illustration 7

Calculate cash price of an asset from the details given below:

	₹
1st instalment payable at the end of 1st Quarter	7,200
2nd instalment payable at the end of 2nd Quarter	6,900
3rd instalment payable at the end of 3rd Quarter	6,600 and
4th instalment payable at the end of 4th Quarter	6,300

Rate of interest is 20% p.a.

Solutions:

Working Note

(a) Per Annum = 4 quarters

(b) When interest p.a. is 20%, interest per quarter must be 5%.

i.e., $20 \times \frac{1}{4} = 5\%$

Calculation of cash price

Date	Working details	Amount ₹
End of 4th quarter	Last instalment due	6,300
	Less: Interest $6,300 \times \frac{5}{105}$	3,00
Beg. of 4th quarter	O/s Balance Add: 3rd quarter instalment	6,000 6,600
		12,600
	Less: Interest	600

(Contd.)

(Contd.)

Beg. of 3rd quarter	O/s Balance $12{,}600\times\frac{5}{105}$	12,000
	Add: 2nd quarter instalment	6,900
		18,900
	Less: interest $18{,}900\times\frac{5}{105}$	900
Beg. of 2nd quarter	O/s Balance	18,000
	Add: 1st quarter instalment	7,200
		25,200
	Less: Interest $25{,}200\times\frac{5}{105}$	1,200
Beg. of 1st quarter	O/s Balance	24,000
Beg. of 1st quarter	Add: Cash down paid	6,000
Beg. of 1st year	Cash price	30,000

III. When the instalments are given exclusive of interest:

Illustration 8

On 1-1-2009 Mr. Anand purchased a Bajaj Scooter from Bharath on HPS. The cash price of the scooter was ₹ 75,000, payable ₹ 15,000 on signing the agreement and the balance in 4 annual instalments of ₹ 15,000 plus interest @ 5% p.a. payable on 31st December, each year. Compute the amount of each instalment payable by Mr. Bharath and also the Hire Purchase Price.

Solution

Calculation of amount of each instalment payable by Mr. Bharath

Date	Working details	Amount ₹
1.1.09	Cash price of scooter	75,000
1.1.09	Less: Down payment made	15,000
1.1.09	O/s Balance	60,000
31.12.09	Add: Interest @ 5% (60,000 × 5/100)	3,000
		63,000
31.12.09	Less: 1st instalment – (15,000 + int 3000)	18,000

(Contd.)

(Contd.)

1.1.10	O/s Balance:	45,000
31.12.10	Add: Interest @ 5% (45000 × 5/100)	2,250
		47,250
31.12.10	Less: 2nd Instalment = (15,000 + 2,250)	17,250
1.1.11	O/s Balance	30,000
31.12.11	Add: Interest @ 5% (30,000 × 5/100)	1,500
		31,500
31.12.11	Less: 3rd instalment (15000 +1500)	16,500
1.1.12	O/s Balance	15,000
31.12.12	Add: Interest @ 5% (15000 × 5/100)	750
		15,750
31.12.12	Less: Last instalment (15000 + 750)	15,750
	Hire purchase price	0

			₹
Amount of each instalment	=	I paid on 31.12.09	18,000
		II paid on 31.12.10	17,250
		III paid on 31.12.11	11,500
		IV paid on 31.12.12	15,750
			67,500
	Add: Cash down paid on 1.1.09		15,000
	∴ Hire purchase price		82,500

Illustration 9

Calculate the value of each instalment from the following:

Cash price = ₹ 60,000; down payment = 30% of the cash price; balance of cash price is payable in 3 equal yearly instalments together with interest @ 5% on the outstanding balance of the cash price.

Solution

Working Notes

(a) Calculation of 3 equal yearly instalments of cash price

	₹
Cash price	60,000
Less: cash down $=\left(\frac{30}{100}\times 60000\right)$	18,000
	42,000

Balance of ₹ 42,000 is payable in 3 equal yearly instalments

∴ each instalment amount exclusive of interest = $\frac{42000}{3}$ years

∴ Each instalment = 14,000

(b) Calculation of amount of Instalment:

Date	Working details	Amount ₹
1.1.1st yr	Cash price	60,000
1.1.1st yr	Less: cash down = 30% of cash price	18,000
1.1.1st yr	O/s Balance	42,000
31.12.1st yr	Add: Interest @ 5% - 42000 × $\frac{5}{100}$	2100
		44,100
31.12.1st yr	Less: 1st instalment (14,000 + 2100)	16,100
1.1.2nd yr	O/s Balance	28,000
31.12.2nd yr	Add: Interest @ 5% 28,000 × $\frac{5}{100}$	1,400
		29,400
31.12.2nd yr	Less: 2nd instalment (14,000 + 1,400)	15,400
1-1-3rd yr	O/s Balance	14,000
31.12.3rd yr	Add: Interest @ 5% (14,000 × $\frac{5}{100}$)	700
		14700
31.12.3rd yr	Less: last instalment (14000 + 700)	14700

1st Instalment	16,100
2nd Instalment	15,400
3rd Instalment	14,700
	46,200
+ Cash Down	18000
HPP	64,200
-CP	60,000
Total interest	4,200

IV. When cash price and instalments are given and rate of interest is not given:

Illustration 10

Cash price of a wagon purchased on 1.1.2010 ₹ 84,000 payable, cash down in signing the agreement ₹ 22,500 and balance in 3 equal annual instalments of ₹ 22,500 each at end of each year.

Calculate hire purchase price and interest included in each instalment.

Solution:

Working notes:

(a) Hire purchase price: Cash down + Amount of instalment × No. of instalments

= 22,500 + 22,500 × 3

∴ HPP = 90,000

(b) Total interest for instalments: HPP – CP

∴ 90,000 – 84,000

Total interest = ₹ 6,000

(c) Calculation of interest included in each instalment :

Instalment due date	No. of Instalments due	Interest =	₹
31.12.2010 31.12.2011 31.12.2012	3 2 1	6,000 × 3/6 = 6,000 × 2/6 = 6,000 × 1/6 =	3,000 2,000 1,000
Total No. of instalments	6	Total interest	6,000

Interest included in	1st instalment	3,000
	2nd instalment	2,000
	3rd instalment	1,000

Illustration 11

A cycle, the cash price of which is ₹ 5,600 is sold on hire purchase system for ₹ 6,400 in four quarterely instalments of ₹ 1,600 each. The first instalment is made at the end of 1st quarter. Show how the interest is calculated.

Solution Working Notes:

(a) Hire purchase price as given in the problem, ₹ 6,400

(b) Cash price as given in the problem ₹ 5,600

(c) Total interest for 4 quarterely instalmetns ₹ 800 (i.e., 6400 – 5600)

(d) Calculation of interest included in each quarterely intalment

Instalment due date	No. of instalments due	Interest =	₹
End of			
1st Qr.	4	800 × 4/10 =	320
2nd Qr.	3	800 × 3/10 =	240
3rd Qr.	2	800 × 2/10 =	160
4th Qr.	1	800 × 1/10 =	80
Total no. of instalments	10	Total interest	800

V. Calculation of cash price with reference to annuity table when the rate of interest and instalments are given:

Under this method, there are three types of problems, namely:

1. When equal instalments are given in the problem
2. When equal instalments and cach down is given in the problem
3. When equal instalments and different annuity values for different years are given.

1. When equal instalments are given in the problem:

Illustration 12

Sri Balaji Transport Company, Bangalore purchases a tempo traveller on hire purchase system over a period of 5 years, payable by annual instalments of ₹ 56,000 each. The seller charges 12% interest p.a. on yearly outstanding balances. The present value of annuity of Re. 1 for 5 years @ 12% interest p.a. is 3.605. Calculate the cash price of the tempo traveller.

Solution

In this problem, amount of all the five instalments payable at end of each year is the same. Therefore, the cash price of the tempo traveller = Instalment × Annuity.

$$= 56{,}000 \times 3.605$$

CP of tempo traveller is ₹ = 2,01,880

2. When equal annual instalments and each down is given in the problem:

Illustration 13

Continuing illustrations No. 12, if cash down given in the problem is ₹ 25,000 in addition to details given on that illustration, then cash price of the tempo traveller is ascertained as follows.

Solution

Cash price of tempo traveller

$$= 56000 \times 3.605 + 25{,}000$$

= 2,01,880 + 25,000
₹ 2,26,880

3. When equal annual instalments and different annuity values for different years are given in the problem:

Illustration 14

Mr. Jayadev purchased a power loom on hire purchase systems paying ₹ 15,000 down and balance in 5 equal annual instalments of ₹ 10,000 each. The rate of interest is 10% p.a. Given the present value of annuity of Re. 1 @ 10% interest for 1st, 2nd, 3rd, 4th & 5th year respectively as 0.909, 0.826, 0.751, 0.683 and 0.621. Calculate cash price of the power loom.

Solution

Cash price of the power loom is calculated as follows:

			₹
1st instalment	=	10,000 × 0.909 =	9.090
2nd instalment	=	10,000 × 0.826	8,260
3rd instalment	=	10,000 × 0.751	7,510
4th instalment	=	10,000 × 0.683	6,830
5th instalment	=	10,000 × 0.621	6,210
+ cash down	=		15,000
		∴ Cash price	52,900

ACCOUNTING PROCEDURE

A. In the books of hire purchaser: (asset accural method)

1. For purchase of an asset on HPS·
   No entry
2. For cash down payment made:-
   Asset A/c Dr.
   To cash / Bank A/c
3. For instalment falling due:
   Asset A/c Dr. (with cash price)
   Interest A/c Dr. (with interest)
   To Hire vendor's A/c
4. For payment of instalment:
   Hire vendor A/c Dr.
   To cash / Bank A/c
5. For depreciation provided on asset:
   Depreciation A/c
   To asset A/c

6. For closing interest A/c and depreciation A/c:-
   Profit and loss A/c Dr.
   To interest A/c
   To depreciation A/c

Note: Entries 3 to 6 have to be continued in subsequent years till payment of the last instalment.

B. In the Books of Hire Vendor:

1. For sale of asset on HPS:
   Hire purchaser's A/c Dr.
   To sales A/c
2. For cash down received:
   Cash / Bank A/c Dr.
   To Hire purchaser's A/c
3. For interest on instalment falling due:
   Hire purchaser's A/c
   To interest A/c
4. For instalment received:
   Cash / Bank A/c Dr.
   To hire purchaser's A/c
5. For closing interest account:
   Interest A/c Dr.
   To P&I A/c

Note: Entries 3 to 5 have to be continued in subsequent years till the receipt of the last instalment.

Illustration 15

On 1st Jan, 2009 a company purchased a wagon on hire purchase system. The cash price of the wagon was ₹ 59,600 and the payment was to be made as follows:

₹ 16,000 were to be paid on the date of agreement and the balance in 3 instalments of ₹ 16,000 each at the end of each year. 5% interest p.a. is charged by the wagon company and the purchaser writes-off depreciation @ 10% p.a. under diminishing balance method. necessary pass the accessory journal entries and prepare necessary ledger A/cs in the books of hire purchaser.

(B.U. Semester Scheme, December, 2006)

Solution:

Working Notes:

(1) Calculation of interest included in each instalment

Date	Working details	Amount ₹
1.1.09	Cash price of wagon	59,600
1.1.09	Less: cash down paid	16,000
1.1.09	O/s Balance	43,600
31.12.09	Add: Interest @ 5% (43,600 × 5/100)	2,180
		45,780
31.12.09	Less: Instalment paid	16,000
1.1.10	O/s Balance	29,780
31.12.10	Add: Interest @ 5% 29,780 × 5/100)	1,489
		31,269
31.12.10	Less: 2nd instalment paid	16,000
1.1.11	O/s Balance	15,269
31.12.11	Add: Interest (16000 – 15269)	731
		16,000
31.12.11	Last instalment paid	16,000
		0

(2) Calculation of depreciation to be provided on wagon (under DB)

Date	Working Details	Amount ₹
1.1.09	Cash price of wagon	59,600
31.12.09	Less: Depreciation @ 10% (59,600 × 10/100)	5,960
1.1.10	O/s Balance of asset	53,640
31.12.10	Less: Depreciation @ 10% (53,640 × 10/100)	5,364
1.1.11	O/s Balance of asset	48,276
31.12.11	Less: Depreciation @ 10% (48,276 × 10/100)	4,828
1.1.12	O/s Balance of asset	43,448

In the Books of hire purchase – Journal entries

Date	Particulars		L.F.	Dr.	Cr.
2009				₹	₹
Jan 1.	Wagon A/c	Dr.		16,000	
	To cash a/c				16,000
	(Being cash down paid on purchase of wagon under HPS)				
Dec. 31.	Wagon A/c	Dr.		13,820	
	Interest A/c	Dr.		2,180	
	To Hire vendor's A/c				16,000
	(Being 1st instalment falling due)				
Dec. 31	Hire vendor's A/c	Dr.		16,000	
	To cash A/c				16,000
	(Being 1st instalment paid)				
Dec. 31	Depreciation A/c	Dr.		5,960	
	To Wagon A/c				5,960
	(Being depreciation provided in asset)				
Dec. 31	Profit and Loss A/c	Dr.		8,140	
	To Interest A/c				2,180
	To Depreciation A/c				5,960
	(Being closure of interest & depreciation a/c)				
2010					
Dec. 31	Wagon account	Dr.		14,511	
	Interest account	Dr.		1,489	
	To hire vendor's A/c				16,000
	(Being 2nd instalment falling due)				
Dec. 31	Hire vendor's A/c	Dr.		16,000	
	To cash A/c				16,000
	(Being 2nd instalment paid)				
Dec. 31	Depreciation A/c	Dr.		5,364	
	To wagon A/c				5,364
	(Being depreciation on asset provided)				
Dec. 31	Profit and Loss A/c	Dr.		6,853	
	To interest A/c				1,489
	To depreciation A/c				5,364
	(Being closure of interest & depreciation a/c)				

(Contd.)

(Contd.)

Date	Particulars	L.F.	Dr.	Cr.
2011				
Dec. 31	Wagon A/c Dr.		15,269	
	Interest A/c Dr.		731	
	To hire vendor's A/c			16,000
	(Being 3rd instalment falling due)			
Dec. 31	Hire vendor's A/c Dr.		16,000	
	To cash A/c			16,000
	(Being 3rd instalment paid)			
Dec. 31	Depreciation A/c Dr.		4,828	
	To wagon A/c			4,828
	(Being depreciation provided for)			
Dec. 31	Profit and loss A/c Dr.		5,559	
	To interest A/c			731
	To depreciation A/c			4,828
	(Being closure of interest & depreciation a/c)			

Ledger A/cs – Books of hire purchaser

Wagon's A/c (Asset A/c)

Dr. Cr.

Date	Particulars	JF	Amount	Date	Particulars	JF	Amount
2009			₹	2009			₹
Jan 1.	To cash A/c		16,000	Dec 31	By depreciation A/c		5,960
Dec 31	To hire vendor's A/c		13,820	Dec 31.	By balance c/d		23,860
			29,820				29,820
2010				2010			
Jan 1	To balance B/d		23,860	Dec 31.	By depreciation A/c		5,364
Dec 31	To hire vendor's A/c		14,511	Dec 31.	By balance c/d		33,007
			38,371				38,371
2011				2011			
Jan 1	To balance B/d		33,007	Dec 31.	By depreciation A/c		4,828
Dec 31	To hire vendor's A/c		15,269	Dec 31.	By balance c/d		43,448
			48,276				48,276
2012							
Jan	To balance B/d		43,448				

Dr. **Hire Vendor's A/c** Cr.

	₹			₹
2009		2009		
Dec 31 To Cash A/c	16,000	Dec 31.	By wagon A/c	13,820
			By interest A/c	2,180
	16,000			16,000
2010		2010		
Dec 31 To Cash A/c	16,000	Dec 31	By wagon A/c	14,511
			By interest A/c	1,489
	16,000			16,000
2011		2011		
Dec 31 To cash A/c	16,000	Dec 31	By wagon A/c	15,269
			By interest A/c	731
	16,000			16,000

Dr. **Interest Account** Cr.

	₹		₹
2009		2009	
Dec 31 To hire vendor's A/c	2,180	Dec 31 By profit & loss A/c	2,180
	2,180		2,180
2010		2010	
Dec 31 To hire vendor's A/c	1,489	Dec 31 By profit & loss A/c	1,489
	1,489		1,489
2011		2011	
Dec 31 To hire vendor's A/c	731	Dec 31 By profit & loss A/c	731
	731		731

Dr. **Depreciation Account** Cr.

	₹		
2009		2009	
Dec 31 To wagon A/c	5,960	Dec 31 By profit & loss A/c	5,960
	5,960		5,960
2010		2010	
Dec 31 To wagon A/c	5,364	Dec 31 By profit & loss A/c	5,364
	5,364		5,364
2011		2011	
Dec 31 To wagon A/c	4,828	Dec 31 By profit & loss A/c	4,828
	4,828		4,828

Illustration – 16

On 1st Jan, 2009 Rama and Company purchased a machinery under hire purchase system. The cash price was ₹ 17,000 payable as under: ₹ 2,000 on signing the agreement and the balance in 3 instalments of ₹ 5,000 each together with interest @ 8% p.a. on 31st of December each year. The asset is depreciated @ 10% p.a. on original cost method.

Give necessary journal entries in the books of hire vendor and also show the ledger accounts necessary.

(B.U. B.Com (S.S.) Dec, 2006)

Solution

Working Notes:

(1) Calculation of interest and amount of instalment

Date	Working Details	Amount
1.1.09	Cash price of machine	17,000
1.1.09	Less: cash down	2,000
1.1.09	O/s Balance:	15,000
31.12.09	Add: Interest – 15,000 × 8/100	1,200
		16,200
31.12.09	1st Instalment (5000 + 1200)	6,200
1.1.10	O/s Balance :	10,000
31.12.10	Add: Interest – 10,000 × 8/100	800
		10,800
31.12.10	Less: 2nd Instalment (5000 + 800)	5,800
1.1.11	O/s Balance :	5,000
31.12.11	Add: Interest – 5,800 × 8/100	400
		5,400
31.12.11	Less: Last instalment (5000 + 400)	5,400
		0
∴	1st instalment – 6200 – interest 1,200 2nd instalment – 5800 – interest 800 3rd instalment – 5400 – interest 400	

(2) Calculation of depreciation : 17,000 × 10/100 = 1,700 p.a.
Since, it is a original cost method of charging depreciations, depreciation remains constant. Hence, ₹ 1,700 p.a. depreciation is to be provided for at the end of each year.

In the books of hire vendor – Journal entries

Date	Particulars	L.F.	Dr.	Cr.
2009			₹	₹
Jan 1	Rama & Co. A/c Dr.		17,000	
	To sales A/c			17,000
	(Being of machinery on H.P.S)			
Jan 1	Cash A/c Dr.		2,000	
	To Rama & Co. A/c			2,000
	(Being cash down received)			
Dec 31	Rama & Co. A/c Dr.		1,200	
	To Interest A/c			1,200
	(Being interest due on 1st instalment)			
Dec 31	Cash A/c Dr.		6,200	
	To Rama & Co. A/c			6,200
	(Being 1st instalment received)			
Dec 31	Interest A/c Dr.		1,200	
	To profit & loss A/c			1,200
	(Being interest A/c closed)			
2010				
Dec 31	Rama & Co. A/c Dr.		800	
	To Interest A/c			800
	(Being interest due on 2nd instalment)			
Dec 31	Cash A/c Dr.		5,800	
	To Rama & Co. A/c			5,800
	(Being 2nd instalment received)			
Dec 31	Interest A/c Dr.		800	
	To profit & loss A/c			800
	(Being interest a/c closed)			
2011				
Dec 31	Rama & Co. A/c Dr.		400	
	To Interest A/c			400
	(Being Interest due on 3rd Instalment)			
Dec 31	Cash A/c Dr.		5,400	
	To Rama & Co. A/c			5,400
	(Being last instalment received)			
Dec 31	Interest A/c Dr.		400	
	To Profit & Loss A/c			400
	(Being Interest A/c closed)			

Ledger Accounts in the books of Hire Vendor
Rama & Co. Account

Dr. **(Hire Purchaser's)** Cr.

Date	Particulars	JF	Amount	Date	Particulars	JF	Amount
2009			₹	2009			₹
Jan 1	To sales A/c		17,000	Jan 1	By cash A/c		2,000
Dec 31	To interest A/c		1,200	Dec 31	By cash A/c		6,200
				Dec 31	By balance c/d		10,000
			18,200				18,200
2010							
Jan 1	To balance B/d		10,000	Dec 31	By cash A/c		5,800
Dec 31	To interest A/c		800	Dec 31	By balance c/d		5,000
			10,800				10,800
2011							
Jan 1	To balance B/d		5,000	Dec 31	By cash A/c		5,400
Dec 31	To interest A/c		400				
			5,400				5,400

Dr. **Interest A/c** Cr.

Particulars	Amount	Date	Particulars	Amount
2009	₹	2009		₹
Dec 31. To P&L A/c	1,200	2009 Dec 31.	By Rama & Co. A/c	1,200
	1,200			1,200
2010				
Dec 31. To P&L A/c	800	Dec 31.	By Rama & Co. A/c	800
	800			800
2011				
Dec 31. To P&L A/c	400	Dec 31.	By Rama & Co. A/c	400
	400			400

Dr. **Sales A/c** Cr.

Particulars	Amount	Date	Particulars	Amount
2009	₹	2009		₹
Dec 31. To trading A/c	17,000	Dec 31	By Cash A/c	17,000
	17,000			17,000

3.8 DEFAULT AND REPOSSESSION

In case if the hire purchaser fails to pay any instalment, hire vendor, being the owner of goods till the payment of the last instalment, can repossess / seize the goods from the hire purchaser and forfeit the amount received so far.

The repossession of the goods may be partial or full, depending on the terms of agreement entered into between the parties – hire purchase and hire vendor.

A. Partial Repossession

In this case, only a part of the amount received from the hire purchaser (i.e., in respect of goods repossessed) can be forfeited and then, some money may have to be incurred to get the seized goods repaired so as to sell them later on.

Calculating of worth of assets: (1) Left with hire purchaser and (2) worth of assets repossessed:

(1) Worth of assets left with hire purchaser:

Calculate the value of asset left with hire purchaser by providing depreciation at normal rate till the date of default.

(2) Worth of assets repossessed:

Value of assets repossessed has to be calculated in the manner specified in the given problem.

Accounting Procedure

In the Books of Hire Purchaser:

With regard to preparation of Asset A/c:

(1) on purchase of asset : Asset A/c Dr. (with cash price) to hire vendor A/c

(2) on providing depreciation at To Hire Vendor's A/c the the end of each year: Depreciation A/c Dr. To Asset A/c.
(Note: Depreciations is to be provided till the date of default).

(3) on repossessing of asset by hire vendor: Hire vendor's A/c Dr. to Asset A/c (with worth of asset taken away)

(4) Find out profit or loss, adopting the procedure given below:

		Amount ₹
Worth of the total asset left with buyer on date of default (A) xxx		
(i.e., total cash price – depreciation up to date of default)		
Less: Depreciation as usual	xxx	
Worth of asset left with the buyer	xxx	
Worth of asset taken away by the seller	xxx	(B) xxx
	Loss	(C) xxx

Note: It is loss when (A) is more 8than (B) and otherwise it is profit.

Entry for accounting loss or profit:

(a) For loss: P&L A/c Dr.
  To asset A/c and

(b) For profit: Asset A/c Dr.
  To P&L A/c

II. With regard to preparation of hire vendor's A/c:

(1) Pass the entries related to hire vendor A/c (i.e., cash down payment, interest due, payment of instalment – as usual) till the date of default.

(2) For asset taken away : Hire vendor's A/c Dr. to Asset A/c

Note: with worth of assets on the date of repossession.

In the books of hire vendor

A. Preparation of hire purchaser's A/c:

(1) Pass the entries as usual till the date of default.

(2) Pass the entry given below, for goods taken away from hire purchase
  Goods Returned A/c Dr.
    To Hire Purchaser's A/c

Note: with worth of assets taken away.

B. Preparation of goods returned A/c:

(1) Pass the entry given below for expenses incurred to get the repossessed goods repaired as:
  Goods Returned A/c Dr.
    To Cash A/c

(2) Entry for sale of repossessed goods: Cash A/c Dr. To goods returned A/c and

(3) Entry for profit or loss on sale of repossessed goods:

(i) For profit: Goods Returned A/c Dr.
  To profit and loss A/c

(ii) For loss: Reverse only

Illustration 17

On 1.1.2010 Mr. Rajanna purchased 4 motor bikes from Suzuki Motors. The cas price of each motor bike was ₹ 35,000. The hire purchase price for all the 4 bikes was ₹ 1,50,000, payable ₹ 37,500 towards down payment and the balance on 3 equal annual instalments of ₹ 37,500 each at the end of each year. Suzuki Motors charged interest @ 5% p.a. Rajanna has provided depreciation @ 10% p.a. fixed instalment method.

Having paid the down payment and first instalment due on 31-12-2010, Rajanna could not pay the 2nd instalment. Leaving one motor bike with Rajanna, Suzuki Motors seized 3 bikes at an agreed value calculated after providing depreciation @ 20% p.a. on diminishing balance method. Suzuki Motors incurred ₹ 3,000 towards repairs of repossessed motor bikes and sold them to Mr. Satish for ₹ 87,500.

Pass the necessary Journal entries to record the above transactions in the books of both Rajanna and Suzuki Motors and also prepare ledger a/c necessary.

Solution:

Working Notes:

(1) Calculation of interest included in each instalment

Date	Working details	Amount ₹
1.1.10	Cash price of 4 M. Bikes (35000 x 4)	1,40,000
1.1.10	Less: cash down payment	37,500
1.1.10	O/s Balance	1,02,500
31-12-10	Add: Interest – 1,02,500 × 5/100	5,125
		1,07,625
31-12-10	Less: Instalment paid	37,500
1-1-11	O/s Balance	70,125
31-12-11	Add: Interest – 70125 × 5/100	3,506
		73,631
31-12-11	Less: 2nd instalment paid	37,500
1-1-12	O/s Balance	36,131
31-12-12	Add: Interest (37500 – 36,131)	1,369
		37,500
31-12-12	Less: Last instalment paid	37,500
		0

Confirmation: HPP – CP = Total interest for instalments
= 1,50,000 – 1,40,000 = ₹ 10,000
10,000 (i.e., 5,125 + 3,506 + 1,369)

(2) Calculation of worth of Motor Bike left with Rajanna (Hire purchase)

	₹
Cash price of 1 Motor Bike	35,000
Less: Depreciations @ 10% for the year 2010 on FIM	3,500
	31,500
Less: Depreciations for 2nd year i.e., 2010 i.e., the date of default	3,500
∴ Worth of M. Bike left with purchaser at end of 2011, the 2nd year	28,000

Note: FIM = Fixed Instalment Method

(3) Calculation of worth of Motor Bikes taken away by Suzuki Motors

	₹
Cash price of 3 Motor Bikes taken away for non-payment of 2nd instalment (35,000 x 3)	1,05,000
Less: Depreciations @ 20% on DBM for the year 2010	21,000
	84,000
Less: Depreciations @ 20% on DBM for 2nd year 2011	16,800
∴ Worth of 3 Motor Bikes taken away by Suzuki Motors at end of 2011, for default in paying 2nd instalment	67,200

Note: DBN = Diminishing Balance Method

Journal entries in the books of hire purchaser – Mr. Rajanna

Date	Particulars	L.F.	Dr.	Cr.
2010				
Jan 1	Motor Bikes A/c Dr.		1,40,000	
	To Suzuki Motors A/c			1,40,000
	(Being purchase of 4 M-Bikes on HPS)			
Jan 1	Suzuki Motors A/c Dr.		37,500	
	To Cash A/c			37,500
	(Being cash down paid)			
Dec 31	Interest A/c Dr.		5,125	
	To Suzuki Motors A/c			5,125
	(Being interest on 1st instalment due)			
Dec 31	Suzuki Motors A/c Dr.		37,500	
	To Cash A/c			37,500
	(Being 1st Instalment paid)			
Dec 31	Depreciation A/c Dr.		14,000	
	To Motor Bikes A/c			14,000
	(Being depreciation provided)			
Dec 31	Profit and Loss A/c Dr.		19.125	
	To Interest A/c			5,125
	To Depreciation A/c			14,000
	(Being closure of Interest and Depreciation A/c)			
2011				
Dec 31	Interest A/c Dr.		3,506	
	To Suzuki Motors A/c			3,506
	(Being interest on 2nd instalment due)			
Dec 31	Suzuki Motors A/c Dr.		67,200	
	To Motor Bikes A/c			67,200
	(Being 3 M-Bikes taken way for default on payment of 2nd instalment)			

(Contd.)

(Contd.)

Date	Particulars	L.F.	Dr.	Cr.
Dec 31	Depreciation A/c Dr.		14,000	
	To Motor Bikes A/c			14,000
	(Being Depreciation provided)			
Dec 31	Profit and Loss A/c Dr.		16,800	
	To Motor Bikes A/c			16,800
	(Being loss on purchase of M-bikes on HPS transferred)			

Ledger Accounts in the book of Hire purchase

Dr. **Motor Bikes Account** Cr.

Date	Particulars	JF	Amount	Date	Particulars	JF	Amount
2010			₹	2010			₹
Jan 1	To Suzuki Mother A/c		1,40,000	Dec. 31	By depreciation A/c		14,000
				Dec. 31	By balance c/d		1,26,000
			1,40,000				1,40,000
2011				2011			
Jan 1	To Balance B/d		1,26,000	Dec 31.	By depreciation a/c		14,000
					By Suzuki Motor		67,200
					By P & L A/c (loss)		16,800
					By Balance c/d		28,000
			1,26,000				1,26,000

Suzuki Motors Account

Dr. (Hire vendor's A/c) Cr.

Date	Particulars	JF	Amount	Date	Particulars	JF	Amount
2010			₹	2010			₹
Jan 1	To cash A/c (down)		37,500	Jan. 1	By Motor Bike A/c		1,40,000
Dec 31	To cash A/c (1st part)		37,500	Dec. 31	By Interest A/c		5,125
	To balance c/d		70,125				
			1,45,125				1,45,125
2011				2011			
Dec. 31	To Motor Bikes A/c (taken away)		67,200	Jan 1.	By Balance B/d		70,125
				Dec. 31	By Interest		5,506
	To Balance c/d*		6,431				
			73,631				73,631

Note: Balance * of ₹ 6431 has to be paid by Mr. Rajanna to Suzuki Motors for having retained one motor bike.

Journal entries in the books of Hire Vendor - Suzuki Motors

Date	Particulars	L.F.	Dr.	Cr.
2010				
Jan 1	Rajana's A/c Dr.		1,40,000	
	To sales A/c			1,40,000
	(Being sale of 4 M-Bikes on HPS)			
Jan 1.	Cash A/c Dr		37,500	
	to Rajanna's A/c			37,500
	(Being cash down received)			
Dec. 31	Rajanna's A/c Dr		5,125	
	To Interest A/c			5,125
	(Being interest on 1st instalment following here)			
Dec. 31	Cash A/c Dr		37,500	
	To Rajanna's A/c			37,500
	(Being 1st installment received			
Dec. 31	Interest A/c Dr		5,125	
	Being intrest A/c closed			
	To profit and loss A/c			5,125
2011				
Dec.31	Rajanna's A/c Dr		3,506	
	To interest A/c			3,506
	(Being interest on 2nd instalment follwoing)			
Dec. 31	Bike Returned A/c Dr		67,200	
	To Rajanna's A/c			67,200
	(Being motor bike taken away for non-payment of 2nd instalment)			
Dec. 31	Motor Bikes Returned A/c Dr		3,000	
	To cash A/c			3,000
	(Being expense incurred to get M-bike repaired)			
Dec. 31	Cash A/c Dr		87500	
	To Motor Bike returned			87500
	(Being re-sale of M-Bikes returned)			
Dec. 31	Motor Bike Returned A/c Dr		17,300	
	To profit & loss A/c			17,300
	(Being profit in resale of (M-bikes transfered)			

(Contd.)

Ledger A/c in the books of hire vendor - Suzuki Motors

Rajannas Accout

Dr. (Hire vendor's A/c) Cr.

Date	Particulars	JF	Amount	Date	Particulars	JF	Amount
2010			₹	2010			₹
Jan 1	To Sales A/c		1,40,000	Jan 1	By Cash A/c		37,500
	To interest A/c		5,125	Dec 31	By Cash A/c		37,500
					By Balance A/c		70,125
			1,45,125				1,45,125
2011				2011			
Jan. 1	To Balance B/d		70,125	Dec 31	By Motor Bike returned A/c		67,200
	To Interest A/c		36,506		Balance c/d		6,431
			73,631				73,631

Dr. **(Motor Bikes Returns A/c)** Cr.

Date	Particulars	Amount	Date	Particulars	Amount
2011		₹	2010		₹
Dec 31	To Rajanna A/c	67,200	Dec 1	By Cash A/c (Sales)	87,500
	To Cash A/c - expenses	3,000			
	To P & L Ac/ - profit	17,300			
		87,500			87,500

FULL OR COMPLETE REPOSSESSION

When the hire vendor takes back the possession of goods completely from hire purchaser for default in payment of any instalment, it is called complete respossession of goods.

Accounting procedure in the books of hire purchase:

1. Firstly, pass all the usual entries till the date of default.
2. Secondly, on the date of default, the balance (o/s) outstanding alongwith interest due for instalment unpaid should be transferred with asset repossessed a/c close hire vendors a/c.
3. Lastly, if there remains any balance in asset a/c transfer it to profit and loss a/c as loss and close the asset a/c.

Note: To order to understand easily the accounting procedure, prepare hire vendor's account first and then prepare asset A/c.

Accounting procedure in the books of hire vendor:

(1) Firstly, pass all the usual entries till the date of default in payment of any instalment.

(2) Secondly, on the date of default, O/s balance along with intrest due for unpaid instalment should be transferred with 'goods returned a/c' and close Hire purchaser's a/c

(3) Thirdly, debit goods returned a/c with expenses incurred to get the repossessed goods repaired passing J/E = goods returned a/c Dr.
   To Cash a/c

(4) Fourthly, pass an entry for sale of repossessed goods cash a/c Dr.
   To goods returned a/c

(5) Lastly tranfer profit/loss passing entry: P & L a/c Dr
   To goods returned A/c
   or reverse entry as the case may be for loss or profit on sale of repossessed goods respectively.

4

Royalty Accounts

SYNOPSIS

4.1 INTRODUCTION

An individual or a firm wishes to make use of some special rights vested with some other persons. Such persons willing to make use of special rights belonging to other person is called a tenant or lessee. The person who happens to be the owner of such special rights is called landlord or lessor. Therefore, 'Royalty' is the sum payable by the lessee to the landlord for making use of special rights vested with the landlord as per the agreement entered into.

4.2 MEANING AND DEFINITION

'Royalty' is the sum payable by one person called 'lessee' to another person called lessor or landlord for making use of special rights belonging to the latter according to the agreement entered into.

Examples

(1) Mining royalties – Where royalty is payable by the lessee to the landlord for raising coal or minerals.

(2) Copyright royalties – Where royalty is payable by a publisher of a book (lessee) to the author of the book for publishing his book.

(3) Patent royalties – Where royalty is payable by a producer or a manufacturer to the owner of the patent right for using his patent.

(4) Oil-well royalty – Where royalty is payable by a person extracting oil from the well to its owner.

(5) Trademark royalty – Where royalty is payable by the user of trademark to its owner.

(6) Brick making royalty – Where royalty is payable by the manufacturer of bricks to the owner of the land where the mud is available for the purpose.

Definitions

William Pickles defines royalty as:

> "Royalty is the remuneration payable to a person in respect of use of an asset, whether hired or purchased from such person, calculated by reference to and varying with quantities produced or sold as a result of such asset."

J.R. Batliboi defines royalty as:

> "The term royalty expresses an amount payable by one, in return for some special right or privilege conceded to him by another person, such as the right to publish a book, or to manufacture and sell a patented article or to work a mine."

Accordingly, the royalty is the sum payable based on output or sale to the owner of mine or a patent or author of a book or any other person possessing some special rights or privileges. In other words, it is the periodic payment payable by a tenant to the owner of some special right or privilege for making use of such rights.

4.3 TECHNICAL TERMS USED

Minimum Rent/Dead Rent /Fixed Rent/Surface Rent/Rock Rent

Minimum or dead rent clause is generally inserted in every royalty agreement for the reason that it takes several years to raises the required quantity of minerals in case of raising royalty or to sell reasonable number of books in case copyright royalty and so on. Hence, this clause is inserted to protect the interest of the owner or landlord in such a way that he should not undergo any loss at the initial stages of lease.

Thus, the minimum rent is the minimum (or fixed) guaranteed amount payable by the lessee to the landlord during the initial stages of lease agreement. In other words, the lessee should pay minimum rent when the actual royalty earned is less than the minimum rent and should pay actual royalty earned when actual royalty earned is more than minimum rent so as to ensure that there is no loss to the landlord in either case.

For example, J.K. International Publishers publishes a book on Financial Accounting @ minimum rent of ₹ 10,000 p.a. and royalty is being payable @ ₹ 5 per book sold and the number of books sold during 1st year is only 500 and second year 2,500. In this case, the publisher has to pay minimum rent of Rs. 10,000 during the first year because royalty earned is only ₹ 2,500 (i.e., 500 × 5). Here, though the royalty earned is ₹ 7,500 less (i.e. 10,000 minimum rent – 2,500 actual royalty) then minimum rent publisher has to pay a minimum rent ₹ 10,000. Similarly, in the 2nd year, the actual royalty earned is ₹ 12,500 (i.e. 2,500 books × ₹ 5) which is more then the minimum rent ₹ 10,000. In this case the publisher has to pay royalty actually earned.

Short Workings or Royalties Suspense

Excess of minimum rent over the actual royalty earned is called 'short workings' or 'royalty suspense'. In the example cited above, during the 1st year, royalty earned is only Rs. 2500 and minimum rent payable is Rs. 10,000. Therefore, short workings are Rs. 7,500, where short workings = Minimum rent – Actual royalty earned (i.e., 10,000 – 2,500).

Surplus

Excess of actual royalty earned over the minimum rent is called 'surplus'. In our example cited above, during the 2nd year of the lease, actual royalty earned is Rs. 12,500 and minimum rent fixed is Rs. 10,000. Hence, Rs. 2500, the excess of royalty over minimum rent, is referred to as surplus.

Recoupment of Short-workings

Recoupment of short-workings means recovery of short-workings or loss, underwent by the lessee during the initial stages of the lease agreement.

In the example cited above, the publisher underwent a loss of Rs. 7,500, by paying minimum rent of Rs. 10,000 though actual royalty earned is Rs. 2,500 during the 1st year of the lease.

So, in order to compensate the publisher, (the lessee) the author of the book (landlord) allows the publisher to recover such loss / short-workings in the years to come, i.e., subsequent years out of surplus within the stipulated period, which is referred to as 'recoupment of short-workings'.

4.4 TREATMENT OF STRIKE/STOPPAGE OF WORK

Sometimes the work may be stopped due to strike or lockout during the period. As a result, the output is reduced during that period or year. Hence, it is generally provided in the royalty agreement that minimum rent has to be reduced proportionally to the period of strike/ lockout or may be provided that the actual royalty earned during the period will discharge the obligation for that period irrespective of the amount of minimum rent fixed.

4.5 RENT AND ROYALTY

Royalty payable is an expenditure to the lessee or tenant as he has to pay it for raising/producing coal, publishing a book, etc. Royalty, therefore, is nominal in nature and is almost synonymous with rent. But there is a lot of difference between them.

The main differences are:

1. Rent is the consideration payable for using some asset – land, building, machinery, etc., whereas royalty is the consideration payable for using some special right / privilege in such tangible asset.
2. Rent is payable according to time, say, per day, per week or per month or per annum as the case may be whereas royalty is payable according to the yield, i.e., output – quantity of coal raised, number books sold, etc.

4.6 ACCOUNTING PROCEDURES

In the books of lessee or tenant.

I method (with minimum rent A/c)	*II method(without minimum rent A/c)*
1. When minimum rent or dead rent is payable: Minimum rent A/c Dr. To landlord A/c 2. When minimum rent A/c is closed: Royalties A/c Dr. Short-workings A/c Dr. To minimum Rent A/c *Note*: The question of paying minimum rent arises only when the actual royalty earned is less than the minimum rent) 3. When minimum rent is paid: Landlord A/c Dr. To Cash / Bank A/c 4. When actual royalty earned is more than N/A payable. Royalties A/c Dr. To landlord A/c 5. When short-workings are recovered: Landlord A/c Dr. To short-workings A/c *Note*: Alternatively, an entry may also be passed by merging entry No. 4 & 5 as :	1. Under this method, an entry may be passed consolidating entry No. 1 & 2 of the 1st method as: Royalties A/c Dr. Short-workings A/c Dr. To landlord A/c *Note*: All other entries to be passed are common under both methods) 2. When minimum rent is paid: Landlord's A/c Dr. To Cash / Bank A/c 3. When actual royalty earned is more than N/R payable: Royalties A/c Dr. To landlord A/c 4. When short-workings are recovered: Landlord A/c Dr. To short workings A/c *Note*: Alternatively, an entry may also be passed by merging entry No. 2 & 3 as: Royalties A/c Dr. To short-workings A/c To landlord A/c

Royalties A/c Dr. To short-workings A/c To landlord A/c 6. When royalties A/c is closed: Profit and loss A/c Dr. To royalties A/c 7. When there is irrecoverable short-workings: Profit and loss A/c Dr. To short-workings A/c *Note:* Alternatively a combined entry i.e., of 6 & 7) can also be passed as: Profit and loss A/c Dr. To royalties A/c To short-workings A/c	5. When royalties A/c closed: Profit and loss A/c Dr. To royalties A/c 6. For irrecoverable short-workings (if any): Profit and loss A/c Dr. To short-workings A/c *Note*: Alternatively, a combined entry (i.e., of 5 and 6) can also be passed as: Profit and loss A/c Dr. To royalties A/c To short-workings A/c

Problems and Solutions

Illustration 1: V.M. Collieries Ltd. took from M/S Bangalore Bros. on lease a coal mine for a period of 20 years from 1st Jan, 2008 at a minimum rent of ₹ 30,000 p.a. merging into a royalty of Rs. 2/- per ton of coal with a power to recoup short- workings over the first 3 years of the lease:

The output for the first 4 years was:

Year	Output. (Tons)
2008	10,000
2009	15,000
2010	17,000 and
2011	20,000 respectively

Draft necessary journal entries in the books of V.M. Collieries Ltd. with minimum rent A/c giving effect to the above transactions and also prepare necessary ledger accounts.

Solution:

Working Note

Before we actually proceed with passing Journal entries, we have to prepare royalties rayable chart in order to ascertain:

(a) When the minimum rent is payable?

(b) When royalties are payable?
(c) When can the lessee recover short-workings and by how much?
(d) What is the amount of short-workings not recovered by the lessee within the stipulated period?

Royalties payable chart

Year	Output (Tons)	Royalty ₹ 2/- Ton	Minimum Rent	Short-workings	Surplus	Short-workings		Amt. payable to landlord
						Recovered	Not recovered	
		₹	₹	₹	₹	₹	₹	
2008	10,000	20,000	30,000	10,000	-	-	-	30,000
2009	15,000	30,000	30,000	-	-	-	-	30,000
2010	17,000	34,000	30,000	-	40,00	4,000	6,000	30,000
2011	20,000	40,000	30,000	-	10,000	-	-	40,000

Where, short-workings can be recovered within 1st 3 years i.e., 2010, and thereafter, the lessee has no power to recomp short-workins.

Journal entries in the books of V.M. Collieries Ltd., (Lessee)

Date	Particulars		L.F.	Dr.	Cr.
2008				₹	₹
Dec. 31	Minimum Rent A/c	Dr.		30,000	
	To Bangalore Bros. A/c (Landlord)				30,000
	(Being Minimum Rent falling due)				
Dec. 31	Royalties A/c	Dr.		20,000	
	Short-workings A/c	Dr.		10,000	
	To Minimum Rent A/c				30,000
	(Being Minimum Rent A/c closed)				
Dec. 31	Bangalore Bros. A/c	Dr.		30,000	
	To Cash A/c				30,000
	(Being Minimum Rent paid)				
Dec. 31	Profit and loss A/c	Dr.		20,000	
	To Royalties A/c				20,000
	(Being Royalties transferred)				

(Contd.)

(Contd.)

2009			
Dec. 31 Royalties A/c Dr.		30,000	
To Bangalore Bros. A/c			30,000
(Being royalties payable)			
Dec. 31 Bangalore Bros. A/c Dr.		30,000	
To cash A/c			30,000
Being royalties paid)			
Dec. 31 Profit and loss A/c Dr.		30,000	
To royalties A/c			30,000
(Being royalties transferred)			
2010			
Dec. 31 Royalties A/c Dr.		34,000	
To Bangalore Bros. A/c			34,000
(Being royalties payable)			
Dec. 31 Landlord's (Bangalore Bros.) A/c Dr.		34,000	
To short-workings			4,000
To cash A/c			30,000
(Being part of the short-workings recovered and the balance is paid)			
Dec. 31 Profit and loss A/c Dr.		40,000	
To royalties A/c			34,000
To short-workings A/c			6,000
(Being royalties and irrecoverable shortworkings transferre)			
2011			
Dec. 31 Royalties A/c Dr.		40,000	
To Bangalore Bros. A/c			40,000
(Being royalties payable)			
Dec. 31 Bangalore Bros. A/c Dr.		40,000	
To bank A/c			40,000
(Being royalties paid)			
Dec. 31 Profit and loss A/c Dr.		40,000	
To royalties A/c			40,000
(Being royalties transferred)			

Ledger accounts in the books of V.M. Collieries Ltd. (Lessee)

Minimum Rent A/c

Dr. Cr.

	₹		₹
2008		2008	
Dec. 31 To Bangalore Bros. A/c	30,000	Dec. 31 By Royalties A/c	20,000
		By Short-workings A/c	10,000
	30,000		30,000

Bangalore Bros. A/c

Dr. Cr.

	₹		₹
2008		2008	
Dec. 31 To cash A/c	30,000	Dec. 31 By minimum rent A/c	30,000
	30,000		30,000
2009		2009	
Dec. 31 To cash A/c	30,000	Dec. 31 By royalties A/c	30,000
	30,000		30,000
2010		2010	
Dec. 31 To short-workings A/c	4,000	Dec. 31 By royalties A/c	34,000
To Cash A/c	30,000		
	34,000		36,000
2011		2011	
Dec. 31 To cash A/c	40,000	Dec. 31 By royalties A/c	40,000
	40,000		40,000

Royalties A/c

Dr. Cr.

	₹		₹
2008		2008	
Dec. 31 To minimum rent A/c	20,000	Dec. 31 By profit and loss A/c	20,000
	20,000		20,000
2009		2009	
Dec. 31 To Bangalore Bros.	30,000	Dec. 31 By profit and loss A/c	30,000
	30,000		30,000
2010		2010	
Dec. 31 To Bangalore Bros. A/c	34,000	Dec. 31 By profit and loss A/c	34,000
	34,000		34,000
2011		2011	
Dec. 31 To Bangalore Bros. A/c	40,000	Dec. 31 By profit and loss A/c	40,000
	40,000		40,000

Short Workings A/c

Dr. Cr.

	₹		₹
2008 Dec. 31 To minimum rent A/c	10,000	2008 Dec. 31 By balance c/d	10,000
	10,000		10,000
2009 Jan. 1 To balance B/d	10,000	2009 Dec. 31 By balance c/d	10,000
	10,000		10,000
2010 Jan. 1 To balance B/d	₹ 10,000	2010 Dec. 31 By Bangalore Bros. By profit and loss A/c	₹ 4,000 6,000
	10,000		10,000

Illustration 2: Sunil took on lease an oil well from Ajay Oil Ltd. on 1.1.2008. The minimum rent was Rs. 2,00,000 and royalty was Rs. 20 per ton of crude oil raised. The short-workings were recoverable in the succeeding 2 years of such short-workings, but on the condition that if during the next year of any short-workings, the lessee is unable to recover the same (either fully/partly), he will lose the right to recover 50% of such unrecovered amount of short-workings. The output during the first 4 years respectively were 5,500; 8,000; 11,250, and 12,500 tons.

Prepare minimum rent A/c, royalty A/c, short-workings A/c and Ajay Oil Ltd. or in the books of Sunil.

(BU. I Semester B.Com. Nov. 2004)

Solution:

Royalties payable chart

Year	Output (tons)	Royalty ₹ 2/- ton	Minimum rent	Short-workings	Surplus	Short-workings		Amt. payable to landlord
						Recovered	Not recovered	
		₹	₹	₹	₹	₹	₹	
2008	5,500	1,10,000	2,00,000	90,000	-	-	-	2,00,000
2009	8,000	1,60,000	2,00,000	40,000	-	-	-	2,00,000
2010	11,250	2,25,000	2,00,000	-	25,000	25,000	65,000	2,00,000
2011	12,500	2,50,000	2,00,000	-	50,000	20,000	20,000	2,30,000

Minimum Rent A/c

Dr.			Cr.
2008	₹	2008	₹
Dec. 31 To Ajay Oil Ltd. (Landlord)	2,00,000	Dec. 31 By royalties A/c	1,10,000
		By short-workings A/c	90,000
	2,00,000		2,00,000
2009		2009	
Dec. 31 To Ajay Oil Ltd.	2,00,000	Dec. 31 By royalties A/c	1,60,000
		By short-workings	40,000
	2,00,000		2,00,000

Royalties A/c

Dr.			Cr.
2008	₹	2008	₹
Dec. 31 To minimum rent A/c	1,10,000	Dec. 31 By profit and loss A/c	1,10,000
	1,10,000		1,10,000
2009		2009	
Dec. 31 To minimum rent A/c	1,60,000	Dec. 31 By profit and loss A/c	1,60,000
	1,60,000		1,60,000
2010		2010	
Dec. 31 To Ajay Oil Ltd., A/c	2,25,000	Dec. 31 By profit and loss A/c	2,25,000
	2,25,000		2,25,000
2011		2011	
Dec. 31 To Ajay Oil Ltd. A/c	2,50,000	Dec. 31 By profit and loss A/c	2,50,000
	2,50,000		2,50,000

Short-workings A/c

Dr.			Cr.
2008		2008	
Dec. 31 To minimum rent A/c	90,000	Dec. 31 By balance c/d	90,000
	90,000		90,000
2009		2009	
Jan. 1 To balance B/d	90,000	Dec. 31 By balance c/d	1,30,000
Dec. 31 To minimum rent A/c	40,000		
	1,30,000		1,30,000

(Contd.)

(Contd.)

2010			2010		
Jan. 1	To balance B/d	1,30,000	Dec. 31	By Ajay Oil Ltd. A/c	25,000
				By profit and loss A/c	65,000
				By balance c/d	40,000
		1,30,000			1,30,000
2011			2011		
Jan. 1	To balance B/d	40,000	Dec. 31	By Ajay Oil Ltd.	20,000
				By profit and loss A/c	20,000
		40,000			40,000

Ajay Oil Ltd. A/c

Dr. Cr.

		₹			₹
2008			2008		
Dec. 31	To cash A/c	2,00,000	Dec. 31	By minimum rent A/c	2,00,000
		2,00,000			2,00,000
2009			2009		
Dec. 31	To cash A/c	2,00,000	Dec. 31	By minimum Rent A/c	2,00,000
		2,00,000			2,00,000
2010			2010		
Dec. 31	To short-workings A/c	25,000	Dec. 31	By Royalties A/c	2,25,000
	To cash A/c	2,00,000			
		2,25,000			2,25,000
2011			2011		
Dec. 31	To short-workings	20,000	Dec. 31	By Royalties A/c	2,50,000
	To cash A/c	2,30,000			
		2,50,000			2,50,000

Illustration 3: Mahesh wrote a book and got it published with M/s Popular Publishers on the terms that royalty will be paid at ₹ 5 per copy sold subject to a minimum rent of ₹ 15,000 with a right of recoupment of short-workings over the first three years of royalty agreement.

From the following details draw up:

(a) Minimum rent A/c

(b) Royalty A/c

(c) Short-workings A/c and (d) Mr. Mahesh's A/c.

Year	No. of copies printed	Closing stock
2008	2,000 copies	100 copies
2009	3,000 copies	200 copies
2010	4,000 copies	400 copies
2011	5,000 copies	500 copies

(B.U. I Sem. B.com. Dec. 2005)

Solution:

Working Notes:

(1) Before we proceed with the preparation of royalties payable chart, to start with we should ascertain number. of copies sold, the missing information; because the royalty is based on number of copies sold.

Year :		No. of copies sold	=	Opening stocks	+	No. of copies printed	–	Closing stocks
2008	=	1,900 copies	=	-Nil-	+	2,000	–	100
2009	=	2,900 copies	=	100	+	3,000	–	200
2010	=	3,800 copies	=	200	+	4,000	–	400
2011	=	4,900 copies	=	400	+	5,000	–	500

Royalties payable chart

Year	No. of copies sold	Royalty ₹ 5% copy	Minimum rent	Short Workings	Surplus	Short workings		Amt. payable to landlord
						Recovered	Not recovered	
		₹	₹	₹	₹	₹	₹	
2008	1,900	9,500	15,000	5,500	-	-	-	15,000
2009	2,900	14,500	15,000	500	-	-	-	15,000
2010	3,800	19,000	15,000	-	4,000	4,000	2,000	15,000
2011	4,900	24,500	15,000	-	9,500	-	-	24,500

Ledger A/cs in the books of M/s Popular Publishers – Lessee

Minimum rent A/c

Dr.			Cr.
	₹		₹
2008 Dec. 31 To Mahesh's A/c	15,000	2008 Dec. 31 By royalties A/c By short-workings A/c	9,500 5,500
	15,000		15,000
2009 Dec. 31 To Mahesh's A/c	15,000	2009 Dec. 31 By royalties A/c By short-workings A/c	14,500 500
	15,000		15,000

Mr. Mahesh's A/c

Dr.			Cr.
	₹		₹
2008 Dec. 31 To cash A/c	15,000	2008 Dec. 31 By minimum rent A/c	15,000
	15,000		15,000
2009 Dec. 31 To cash A/c	15,000	2009 Dec. 31 By minimum rent A/c	15,000
	15,000		15,000
2010 Dec. 31 To cash A/c To short-workings A/c	15,000 4,000	2010 Dec. 21 By royalties	19,000
	19,000		19,000
2011 Dec. 31 To cash A/c	24,500	2011 Dec. 31 By royalties	24,500
	24,500		24,500

Royalties A/c

Dr.			Cr.
	₹		₹
2008 Dec. 31 To minimum rent A/c	9,500	2008 Dec. 31 By profit & loss A/c	9,500
	9,500		9,500
2009 Dec. 31 To minimum rent A/c	14,500	2009 Dec. 31 By profit & loss A/c	14,500
	14,500		14,500

(Contd.)

(Contd.)

2010			2010		
Dec. 31	To Mahesh's A/c	19,000	Dec. 31	By profit & loss A/c	19,000
		19,000			19,000
2011			2011		
Dec. 31	To Mahesh's A/c	24,500	Dec. 31	By profit & loss A/c	24,500
		24,500			24,500

Short-workings A/c

Dr. Cr.

		₹			₹
2008			2008		
Dec. 31	To minimum rent A/c	5,500	Dec. 31	By balance c/d	5,500
		5,500			5,500
2009			2009		
Jan. 1	To balance B/d	5,500	Dec. 31	By balance c/d	6,000
Dec. 31	To minimum rent A/c	500			
		6,000			6,000
2010			2010		
Jan. 1	To balance B/d	6,000	Dec. 31	By Mahesh's A/c	4,000
				By profit & loss A/c	2,000
		6,000			6,000

Illustration 4: (Problems on without minimum rent A/c)
Jaishree obtained on lease a granite bearing land on 1st Jan 2008, the terms being a royalty of Rs. 700/- per metre granite raised subject to a minimum rent of Rs. 20,00,000 per annum, with a right to recoup short-workings over the 1st three years of lease. The following are the particulars:

Year	Sales in metres	Closing stocks in Metres
2008	2,200 metres	300 metres
2009	3,300 metres	500 metres
2010	4,800 metres	600 metres
2011	6,000 metres	700 metres

You are required to pass Journal entries necessary to record the above in the books of Jaishree. Prepare Royalty A/c, Short-workings A/c and Landlord A/c

(B.U. I Sem. B.Com., Dec. 2007)

Solution:

Working Note:

As the royalty is based on the number of meters raised, we have to calculate number of metres of granite (not given in the problem) raised.

Year	No. of metres of granite raised	=	No. of granite metre sold	+	Closing stock	–	Opening stock
2008	2,500 metres	=	2,200	+	300	-	-NIL-
2009	3,500 metres	=	3,300	+	500	–	300
2010	4,900 metres	=	4,800	+	600	–	500
2011	6,100 metres	=	6,000	+	700	–	600

Royalties payable chart

Year	Output metres	Royalty @ 700 m	Minimum rent	Short-workings	Surplus	Short-workings		Amt. payable to landlord
						recovered	Not recovered	
		₹	₹	₹	₹	₹	₹	₹
2008	2,500	17,50,000	20,00,000	2,50,000	-	-	-	20,00,000
2009	3,500	24,50,000	20,00,000	-	4,50,000	2,50,000	-	22,00,000
2010	4,900	34,30,000	20,00,000	-	14,30,000	-	-	34,30,000
2011	6,100	42,70,000	20,00,000		22,70,000			42,70,000

Journal entries in the books of Jaishree

Date	Particulars		L.F.	Dr.	Cr.
2008					
Dec. 31	Royalties A/c	Dr.		17,50,000	
	Short-workings A/c	Dr.		2,50,000	
	To landlord's A/c				20,00,000
	(Being minimum rent payable)				
2008					
Dec. 31	Landlord's A/c	Dr.		20,00,000	
	To cash A/c				20,00,000
	(Being minimum rent paid)				

(Contd.)

(Contd.)

2008				
Dec. 31	Profit and loss A/c Dr.		17,50,000	
	To royalties A/c			17,50,000
	(Being royalties transferred)			
2009				
Dec. 31	Royalties A/c Dr.		24,50,000	
	To landLord's A/c			24,50,000
	(Being royalties payable)			
Dec. 31	Landlord's A/c Dr.		24,50,000	
	To short-workings A/c			2,50,000
	To cash A/c			22,00,000
	(Being s/ws recovered & balance paid)			
Dec. 31	Profit and loss A/c Dr.		24,50,000	
	To royalties A/c			24,50,000
	(Being royalties transferred)			
2010				
Dec. 31	Royalties A/c Dr.		34,30,000	
	To landlord's A/c			34,30,000
	Being royalties payable)			
Dec. 31	Landlord's A/c Dr.		34,30,000	
	To cash A/c			34,30,000
	(Being royalties paid)			
Dec. 31	Profit and loss A/c Dr.		34,30,000	
	To royalties A/c			34,30,000
	(Being royalties transferred)			
2011				
Dec. 31	Royalties A/c Dr.		42,70,000	
	To landlord's A/c			42,70,000
	(Being royalties payable)			
Dec. 31	Landlord's A/c Dr.		42,70,000	
	To cash A/c			42,70,000
	(Being royalties paid)			
Dec. 31	To profit and loss A/c Dr.		42,70,000	
	To royalties A/c			42,70,000
	(Being royalties transferred)			

Ledger accounts in the books of Jayashree

Royalties A/c

Dr. Cr.

		₹			₹
2008			2008		
Dec. 31	To Landlord's A/c	17,50,000	Dec. 31	By Profit & Loss A/c	17,50,000
		17,50,000			17,50,000
2009			2009		
Dec. 31	To Landlord's A/c	24,50,000	Dec. 31	By Profit & Loss A/c	24,50,000
		24,50,000			24,50,000
2010			2010		
Dec. 31	To Landlord's A/c	34,30,000	Dec. 31	By Profit & Loss A/c	34,30,000
		34,30,000			34,30,000
2011			2011		
Dec. 31	To Landlord's A/c	42,70,000	Dec. 31	By Profit & Loss A/c	42,70,000
		42,70,000			42,70,000

Short-workings A/c

Dr. Cr.

		₹			₹
2008			2008		
Dec. 31	To Landlord's A/c	2,50,000	Dec. 31	By Balance c/d	2,50,000
		2,50,000			2,50,000
2009			2009		
Jan. 1	To Balance B/d	2,50,000	Dec. 31	By Landlord's A/c	2,50,000
		2,50,000			2,50,000

Landlord's A/c

Dr. Cr.

		₹			₹
2008			2008		
Dec. 31	To Cash A/c	20,00,000	Dec. 31	By Royalties A/c	17,50,000
				By Short-workings A/c	2,50,000
		20,00,000			20,00,000
2009			2009		
Dec. 31	To Cash A/c	22,00,000	Dec. 31	By Royalties A/c	24,50,000
	To Short-workings A/c	2,50,000			
		24,50,000			24,50,000

(Contd.)

(Contd.)

2010 Dec. 31	To cash A/c	34,30,000	2010 Dec. 31	By Royalties A/c	34,30,000
		34,30,000			34,30,000
2011 Dec. 31	To Cash A/c	42,70,000	2011 Dec. 31	By Royalties A/c	42,70,000
		42,70,000			42,70,000

Illustration 5: (With floating minimum rent and recoupment of short-workings throughout the terms of lease).

N.N. Co. Ltd., took on lease a mine for a period 25 years from M/s Coal Mines Ltd., at an annual dead rent of Rs. 8,000 for the first year, ₹ 10,000 for the second year and Rs. 12,000 per year thereafter, subject to a royalty of Rs. 2 per ton of coal raised. Excess of minimum rent over royalty in any year could be recouped throughout the term of the lease. The production for the first 5 years was as follows:

Year	2007	2008	2009	2010	2011
Output (tons)	2,500	4,000	5,000	7,000	8,000

You are required to prepare: (1) Dead rent A/c, (2) M/s Coal Mines Ltd., A/c, (3) Royalties A/c and Short-workings A/c.

Solution:

Royalties payable chart

Year	Output (Tons)	Royalty ₹ 2/- Ton	Minimum Rent	Short-workings	Surplus	Short-workings		Amt. payable to landlord
						Recovered	Not recovered	
		₹	₹	₹	₹	₹	₹	₹
2007	2,500	5,000	8,000	3,000	-	-	-	8,000
2008	4,000	8,000	10,000	2,000	-	-	-	10,000
2009	5,000	10,000	12,000	2,000	-	-	-	12,000
2010	7,000	14,000	12,000	-	2,000	2,000	-	12,000
2011	8,000	16,000	12,000	-	4,000	4,000	-	12,000

Dead rent A/c

Dr.		₹		Cr.	₹
2007			2007		
Dec. 31	To M/s Coal Mines Ltd.	8,000	Dec. 31	By royalties A/c	5,000
				By short-workings A/c	3,000
		8,000			8,000
2008			2008		
Dec. 31	To M/s Coal Mines Ltd.	10,000	Dec. 31	By royalties A/c	8,000
				By short-workings A/c	2,000
		10,000			10,000
2009			2009		
Dec. 31	To M/s Coal Mines Ltd.	12,000	Dec. 31	By royalties A/c	10,000
				By short-workings A/c	2,000
		12,000			12,000

M/s Coal Mines Ltd. (Land Lord) A/c

Dr.		₹		Cr.	₹
2007			2007		
Dec. 31	To cash A/c	8,000	Dec. 31	By dead rent A/c	8,000
		8,000			8,000
2008			2008		
Dec. 31	To cash A/c	10,000	Dec. 31	By dead rent A/c	10,000
		10,000			10,000
2009			2009		
Dec. 31	To cash A/c	12,000	Dec. 31	By dead rent A/c	12,000
		12,000			12,000
2010			2010		
Dec. 31	To short-workings A/c	2,000	Dec. 31	By royalties A/c	14,000
	To cash A/c	12,000			
		14,000			14,000
2011			2011		
Dec. 31	To short-workings A/c	4,000	Dec. 31	By royalties A/c	16,000
	To cash A/c	12,000			
		16,000			16,000

Royalties A/c

Dr.			Cr.
2007	₹	2007	₹
Dec. 31 To dead rent A/c	5,000	Dec. 31 By profit and loss A/c	5,000
	5,000		5,000
2008		2008	
Dec. 31 To dead rent A/c	8,000	Dec. 31 By profit and loss A/c	8,000
	8,000		8,000
2009		2009	
Dec. 31 To dead A/c	10,000	Dec. 31 By profit and loss A/c	10,000
	10,000		10,000
2010		2010	
Dec. 31 To M/s Coal Mines Ltd. A/c	14,000	Dec. 31 By profit and loss A/c	14,000
	14,000		14,000
2011		2011	
Dec. 31 To M/s Coal Mines Ltd. A/c	16,000	Dec. 31 By profit and loss A/c	16,000
	16,000		16,000

Short-workings A/c

Dr.			Cr.
2007	₹	2007	₹
Dec. 31 To dead rent A/c	3,000	Dec. 31 By balance c/d	3,000
	3,000		3,000
2008		2008	
Jan. 1 To balance B/d	3,000	Dec. 31 By balance c/d	5,000
Dec. 31 To dead rent A/c	2,000		
	5,000		5,000
2009		2009	
Jan. 1 To balance B/d	5,000	Dec. 31 By balance c/d	7,000
Dec. 31 To dead rent A/c	2,000		
	7,000		7,000

(Contd.)

(Contd.)

2010 Jan. 1	To balance B/d	7,000	2010 Dec. 31	By M/s Coal Mines Ltd. A/c	2,000
				By balance c/d	5,000
		7,000			7,000
2011 Jan. 1	To balance B/d	5,000	2011 Dec. 31	By M/s Coal India Ltd. A/c	4,000
				By balance c/d	1,000
		5,000			5,000
2012 Jan. 1	To balance B/d	1,000			

Illustration 6: (Penalty Clause in Royalty Agreement without Minimum Rent A/c) Gajendran wrote a book and got it published with I.K. International Publishers on the following terms:-

(a) Royalty would be 15% of sale proceeds each year.
(b) Minimum payment of Rs. 10,000 per annum.
(c) Gajendran to revise the book when requested by the publisher and submit to the revised edition within 6 months. If Gajendran delays beyond 6 months, he has to pay publisher penalty @ Rs. 500 per month for the period of delay. Further, in the year of delay, minimum payment was not to apply.

Number of copies sold and sale price of each copy were as follows:

Year	2009	2010	2011
No. of copies sold	2,000	4,000	2,000
Price per copy	₹ 20	₹ 20	₹ 25

At the end of 2010 the 2nd year, Gajendran was requested to revise the book. The revised manuscript reached the publisher on 1st Oct. of 2011, the 3rd year.

Give Journal entries in the books of the publisher.

(B.U. Non-sem. Scheme 1989 modified)

Solution:

Working Notes:

(1) Publisher requested author, Gajendran at end of 2nd year 2010 to revise the book, i.e., from 1st Jan to 30th June of 2011. Had he revised and submitted within June 30th, no penalty could have been imposed. However,

there is a delay of 3 months i.e., 1st July to Ist October. As such, the publisher can reduce Rs. 1,500 (Rs. 500 × 3 months) from royalty payable to the author.

(2) In the year of delay, i.e., 2011, the third year, minimum rent clause does not apply as such, actual royalty earned discharges all obligations.

(3) Nothing is stated about the recoupment of short-workings. Hence, the short-workings of an year should be transferred as loss to profit and loss or assuming that there is no clauses inserted in lease agreement regarding recoupment of short-workings.

Royalties payable chart

Year	No. of book sold	Royalty 15% sale	Mini-mum rent	Short-work-ings	Surplus	Short-workings		Amt. payable to landlord
						Reco-vered	Not reco-vered	
		₹	₹	₹	₹	₹	₹	₹
2009	2,000	6,000	10,000	4,000	-	-	4,000	10,000
2010	4,000	12,000	10,000	-	2,000	-	-	12,000
2011	2,000	7,500	10,000	-	-	-	-	7,500

(4) Royalty is 15% of sales = 2009 = (2000 × 20) 40,000 × 15% = 6,000

2010 = (4000 × 20) 80,000 × 15% = 12,000

2011 = (2000 × 25) 50,000 × 15% = 7,500

(5) Royalty payable for 2011 = Rs. 7,500 – 1,500 penalty recoverable for 3 months delay. Rs. 6,000 is therefore, payable to Gajendran.

In the books of M/s I.K. Publishers

Date	Particulars		L.F.	Dr. ₹	Cr. ₹
2009					
Dec. 31	Royalties A/c	Dr.		6,000	
	Short-workings A/c	Dr.		4,000	
	To Gajendran's A/c				10,000
	(Being M/R payable)				
Dec. 31	Gajendran's A/c (landlord)	Dr.		10,000	
	To cash A/c				10,000
	(Being M/R paid)				

(Contd.)

(Contd.)

Dec. 31	Profit and loss A/c Dr.		10,000	
	To royalties A/c			6,000
	To short-workings A/c			4,000
	(Being royalties and short-workings irrecovered transferred)			
2010				
Dec. 31	Royalties A/c Dr.		12,000	
	To Gajendran's A/c			12,000
	(Being royalties payable)			
Dec. 31	Gajendran's A/c		12,000	
	To cash A/c			12,000
	(Being royalties paid)			
Dec. 31	Profit and loss A/c Dr.		12,000	
	To royalties A/c			12,000
	(Being royalties transferred)			
2011				
Dec. 31	Royalties A/c Dr.		7,500	
	To Gajendran's A/c			7,500
	(Being royalties payable)			
Dec. 31	Gajendran's A/c Dr.		7,500	
	To damages (penalty) recovered A/c			1,500
	To cash A/c			6,000
	(Being penalty for delay in revising the book withhold & the balance is paid)			
Dec. 31	Profit and loss A/c Dr.		7,500	
	To royalties A/c			7,500
	(Being royalties transferred)			
Dec. 31	Damages recovered A/c Dr.		1,500	
	To profit and loss A/c			1,500
	(Being penalty imposed for delay in revision of books transferred)			

Illustration 7: (Strike period – 40% decrease in minimum rent)
Jai Bharath Mining Co2 holds on lease a mine for a period of 20 years commencing from 1.1.2006. According to the lease agreement, the company is to pay Rs. 2/- per ton as royalty with a minimum rent of Rs. 40,000 a year. Short-workings can however, be recovered out of next 2 years only. In the year of strike, the minimum rent is to be reduced to 60%. The output for six years has been given as under:

Year	Output (Tons)
2006	10,000
2007	12,000
2008	28,000
2009	25,000
2010	50,000
2011	15,000 (Strike period)

There was a strike in the 6th year, 2011. Show Landlord A/c and Short-workings A/c.

Solution:

Year	Output (tons)	Royalty ₹ 2/- ton	Minimum rent	Short Workings	Surplus	Short workings		Amt. payable to landlord
						Recovered	Not recovered	
	₹	₹	₹	₹	₹	₹	₹	₹
2006	10,000	20,000	40,000	20,000	-	-	-	40,000
2007	12,000	24,000	40,000	16,000	-	-	-	40,000
2008	28,000	56,000	40,000	-	16,000	16,000	4,000	40,000
2009	25,000	50,000	40,000	-	10,000	10,000	6,000	40,000
2010	50,000	1,00,000	40,000	-	60,000	-	-	1,00,000
Strike 2011	15,000	30,000	24,000	-	6,000	-	-	30,000

Note: 2011 Strike period. ∴ Minimum Rent – $40{,}000 \times \frac{60}{100} = 24{,}000$

In the books of Jai Bharath Mining Co.

Landlord's A/c

Dr. Cr.

	₹		₹
2006		2006	
Dec. 31 To cash A/c	40,000	Dec. 31 By royalties A/c	20,000
		By short-workings A/c	20,000
	40,000		40,000

(Contd.)

(Contd.)

2007 Dec. 31 To cash A/c	40,000	2007 Dec. 31 By royalties A/c By short-workings A/c	24,000 16,000
	40,000		40,000
2008 Dec. 31 To cash A/c To short-workings A/c	40,000 16,000	2008 Dec. 31 By royalties A/c	56,000
	56,000		56,000
2009 Dec. 31 To cash A/c To short-wrokings A/c	40,000 10,000	2009 Dec. 31 By royalties A/c	50,000
	50,000		50,000
2010 Dec. 31 To cash A/c	1,00,000	2010 Dec. 31 By royalties A/c	1,00,000
	1,00,000		1,00,000
2011 Dec. 31 To cash A/c	30,000	2011 Dec. 31 By royalties A/c	30,000
	30,000		30,000

Short-workings A/c

Dr. Cr.

	₹		₹
2006 Dec. 31 To landlord A/c	20,000	2006 Dec. 31 By Balance c/d	20,000
	20,000		20,000
2007 Jan. 1 To balance B/d Dec. 31 To landlord's A/c	20,000 16,000	2007 Dec. 31 By balance c/d	36,000
	36,000		36,000
2008 Jan. 1 To Balance B/d	36,000	2008 Dec. 31 By landlord's A/c By profit and loss A/c By balance c/d	16,000 4,000 16,000
	36,000		36,000
2009 Jan 1. To Balance B/d	16,000	2009 Dec. 31 By landlord's A/c By profit and loss A/c	10,000 6,000
	16,000		16,000

Illustration 8: (When there is strike period and minimum rent is reduced proportionately)

Coal company has taken on lease coal from 'Y' on the following terms:

(a) Lease is for 99 years.

(b) Lease rent is to be 50 paise per annum for every ton of coal raised.

(c) Minimum royalty per annum to be Rs. 30,000; the lessee has a right to recoup any short-workings within a period of 3 years for which the excess payment was made.

(d) In case the working of mines was affected by any strike or riot and there were no raisings, then the minimum rent payable would abate proportionally.

(e) The following were the raisings for the different years:-

Year:	2006	2007	2008	2009	2010	2011
Output:	20,000 tons	35,000 tons	30,000 tons	70,000 tons	80,000 tons	1,00,000 tons

(f) There was a strike in 2008 for 3 months during which no coal was raised)

You are required to show:

(a) Royalties A/c (b) Landlords A/c and (c) Short-workings A/c in the books of 'X' Coal Company.

(C.A. Inter, Nov. 1977—adopted)

Solution:

Working Note:

(1) Excess of M/R over royalty (i.e., S/W) – is to be recouped within a period of 3 following or subsequent years.

(2) M/R for strike period – to be reduced/abated proportionately.

Therefore, minimum rent for strike period – 2008 = $30,000 \times \frac{9}{12} = 22,500$

Royalties payable chart

Year	Output (tons)	Royalty 50 ton	Minimum rent	Short-workings	Surplus	Short-workings Recovered	Short-workings Not recovered	Amt. payable to landlord
		₹	₹	₹	₹	₹	₹	₹
2006	20,000	10,000	30,000	20,000	-	-	-	30,000
2007	35,000	17,500	30,000	12,500	-	-	-	30,000
Strike 2008	30,000	15,000	22,500	7,500	-	-	-	22,500

(Contd.)

(Contd.)

2009	70,000	35,000	30,000	-	5,000	5,000	15,000	30,000
2010	80,000	40,000	30,000	-	10,000	10,000	2,500	30,000
2011	1,00,000	50,000	30,000	-	20,000	7,500	-	42,500

In the books of X-Coal Company

Royalties Account

Dr. Cr.

	₹		₹
2006 Dec. 31 To Y's A/c (Landlord)	10,000	2006 Dec. 31 By profit and loss A/c	10,000
2007 Dec. 31 To Y's A/c	17,500	2007 Dec. 31 By profit and loss A/c	17,500
2008 Dec. 31 To Y's A/c	15,000	2008 Dec. 31 By profit and loss A/c	15,000
2009 Dec. 31 To Y's A/c	35,000	2009 Dec. 31 By profit and loss A/c	35,000
2010 Dec. 31 To Y's A/c	40,000	2010 Dec. 31 By profit and loss A/c	40,000
2011 Dec. 31 To Y's A/c	50,000	2011 Dec. 31 By profit and loss A/c	50,000

Y's Account

Dr. Cr.

	₹		₹
2006 Dec. 31 To cash A/c	30,000	2006 Dec. 31 By royalties A/c By short-workings A/c	10,000 20,000
	30,000		30,000
2007 Dec. 31 To cash A/c	30,000	2007 Dec. 31 By royalties A/c By short-workings	17,500 12,500
	30,000		30,000
2008 Dec. 31 To cash A/c	22,500	2008 Dec. 31 By royalties A/c By short-workings A/c	15,000 7,500
	22,500		22,500

(Contd.)

(Contd.)

2009			2009		
Dec. 31	To short-workings A/c	5,000	Dec. 31	By royalties A/c	35,000
	To cash A/c	30,000			
		35,000			35,000
2010			2010		
Dec. 31	To short-workings A/c	10,000	Dec. 31	By royalties A/c	40,000
	To cash A/c	30,000			
		40,000			40,000
2011			2011		
Dec. 31	To short-workings A/c	7,500	Dec. 31	By royalties A/c	50,000
	To cash A/c	42,500			
		50,000			50,000

Short-workings A/c

Dr. Cr.

		₹			₹
2006			2006		
Dec. 31	To Y's A/c	20,000	By Balance c/d		20,000
2007			2007		
Jan. 1	To Balance B/d	20,000	Dec. 31	By Balance c/d	32,500
Dec. 31	To Y's A/c	12,500			
		32,500			32,500
2008			2008		
Jan. 1	To Balance B/d	32,500	Dec. 31	By Balance c/d	40,000
	To Y's A/c	7,500			
		40,000			40,000
2009			2009		
Jan. 1	To Balance B/d	40,000	Dec. 31	By Y's A/c	5,000
				By profit & loss A/c	15,000
				By balance c/d	20,000
		40,000			40,000
2010			2010		
Jan. 1	To Balance B/d	20,000	Dec. 31	By Y's A/c	10,000
				By profit & loss A/c	2,500
				By balance c/d	7,500
		20,000			20,000

(Contd.)

(Contd.)

2011			2011		
Jan. 1	To balance B/d	7,500	Dec. 31	By Y's A/c	7,500
		7,500			7,500

Illustration 9: On 1st January 2007, Bright Ltd., patentees of a new type of gas burner, issued a licence to Popular Ltd., for the manufacture and sale of burners for 5 years on the following terms:

(a) Popular Ltd., to pay a royalty of Rs. 100 for every burner manufactured subject to a minimum rent of Rs. 50,000 per annum.

(b) If, in any year, royalties calculated on burners manufactured amount to less than the minimum rent, Popular Ltd., may recoup the short-workings against royalties payable in excess of minimum rent in the next year only, but not afterwards.

(c) Payment to be made on 31st December.

Sales and closing stock of burners for 5 years were:-

Year	Sales	Stock on 31st December
2007	200 burners	50 burners
2008	400 burners	100 burners
2009	600 burners	70 burners
2010	550 burners	150 burners
2011	230 burners	20 burners

You are required to show:

(1) Royalties A/c,

(2) Short-workings A/c,

(3) Bright Ltd.'s A/c and

(4) Minimum rent A/c in the books of Popular Ltd., who close their account on 31st December, each year.

(I.C.W.A., Inter June 1987)

Solution:

Working Note:

Before we proceed with the preparation of ledger accounts, first, we have to ascertain the missing information as to the number burners manufactured each year, without which we cannot prepare royalties payable chart. The reason being, royalty is based on the number of burners manufactured.

Therefore, number of burners manufactured is calculated as follows: the number of burners manufactured each year = No. of burners sold + Closing stock – Opening stock

Year	No. of burners sold	+	Closing stock	–	Opening stock	=	No. burners manufactured
2007	200	+	50	–	Nil	=	250
2008	400	+	100	–	50	=	450
2009	600	+	70	–	100	=	570
2010	550	+	150	–	70	=	630
2011	230	+	20	–	150	=	100

Royalties Payable Chart

Year	Output No. of burner manufa-ctureed	Royalty 100/ burner	Mini-mum rent	Short-work-ings	Surplus	Short-workings		Amt. payable to landlord
						Reco-vered	Not reco-vered	
		₹	₹	₹	₹	₹	₹	₹
2007	250	25,000	50,000	25,000	-	-	-	50,000
2008	450	45,000	50,000	5,000	-	-	25,000	50,000
2009	570	57,000	50,000	-	7,000	5,000	-	52,000
2010	630	63,000	50,000	-	13,000	-	-	63,000
2011	100	10,000	50,000	40,000	-	-	-	50,000

In the books of Popular Ltd.

Minimum rent A/c

Dr. Cr.

	₹		₹
2007		2007	
Dec. 31 To landlord A/c (Bright Ltd.)	50,000	Dec. 31 By royalties A/c	25,000
		By Short-workings	25,000
	50,000		50,000
2008		2008	
Dec. 31 To Bright Ltd. A/c	50,000	Dec. 31 By royalties A/c	45,000
		By short-workings	5,000
	50,000		50,000

(Contd.)

(Contd.)

2009 Dec. 31 To Bright Ltd.	50,000	2009 Dec. 31 By royalties A/c	10,000
		By short-workings	40,000
	50,000		50,000

Bright Ltd., A/c

Dr. Cr.

	₹		₹
2007 Dec. 31 To cash A/c	50,000	2007 Dec. 31 By minimum rent A/c	50,000
	50,000		50,000
2008 Dec. 31 To cash A/c	50,000	2008 Dec. 31 By minimum rent A/c	50,000
	50,000		50,000
2009 Dec. 31 To cash A/c	52,000	2009 Dec. 31 By royalties A/c	57,000
To short-workings A/c	5,000		
	57,000		57,000
2010 Dec. 31 To cash A/c	63,000	2010 Dec. 31 By royalties A/c	63,000
	63,000		63,000
2011 Dec. 31 To cash A/c	50,000	2011 Dec. 31 By minimum rent A/c	50,000
	50,000		50,000

Royalties A/c

Dr. Cr.

	₹		₹
2007 Dec. 31 To Minimum Rent A/c	25,000	2007 Dec. 31 By Profit & Loss A/c	25,000
	25,000		25,000
2008 Dec. 31 To Minimum Rent A/c	45,000	2008 Dec. 31 By Profit & Loss A/c	45,000
	45,000		45,000

(Contd.)

(Contd.)

2009 Dec. 31 To Bright Ltd., A/c	57,000	2009 Dec. 31 By Profit & Loss A/c	57,000
	57,000		57,000
2010 Dec. 31 To Bright Ltd.	63,000	2010 Dec. 31 By Profit & Loss A/c	63,000
	63,000		63,000
2011 Dec. 31 To Minimum Rent A/c	10,000	2011 Dec. 31 By Profit & Loss A/c	10,000
	10,000		10,000

Short-workings A/c

Dr. Cr.

	₹		₹
2007 Dec. 31 To Minimum Rent A/c	25,000	2007 Dec. 31 By Balance c/d	25,000
	25,000		25,000
2008 Jan. 1 To Balance B/d Dec. 31 To Minimum Rent A/c	25,000 5,000	2008 Dec. 31 By Profit & Loss A/c By Balance c/d	25,000 5,000
	30,000		30,000
2009 Dec. 31 To Balance B/d	5,000	2009 Dec. 31 By Bright Ltd. A/c	5,000
	5,000		5,000
2011 Dec. 31 To Minimum Rent A/c	40,000	2011 Dec. 31 By Balance c/d	40,000
	40,000		40,000
2012 Jan. 1 To Balance B/d	40,000		

Illustration 10: (When there is strike as well as lock-out period)

Nag Bros. obtained a lease of a coal mine on 1st April 2006 on the following terms:

(a) Royalty Re 1 per ton
(b) Minimum rent Rs. 12,000 p.a.
(c) Recoupment of short-workings of each year during next 3 years subject to a Rs. 2,500 p.a.
(d) In the event of strike, the minimum rent would be taken pro-rata on the basis of actual working days, but in the event of lock-out, the lessor

would enjoy the concession in respect of minimum rent for 50% of the period of lock-out.

(e) Working for the first 5 years is as follows:

Year	Actual royalty
2006-07	7,000
2007-08	10,200
2008-09	19,000
2009-10	10,800 (Strike 73 days)
2010-11	9,000 (Lock-out – 4 months)

Show:

(1) Minimum rent A/c
(2) Landlord's A/c
(3) Short-workings A/c and
(4) Royalties A/c in the books of Nag Bros.

(Adapted from Madurai Kansraj University)

Solution:

Working Notes:

(1) Calculation of minimum rent for the year of strike:

		₹
=	M/R per year =	12,000
	Less: M/R for 73 days of strike: $= 12,000 \times \frac{73}{365}$	2,400
		9,600

Min. rent for year of strike - (2009-10)

(2) Minimum rent for the period of lock-out = ?

M/R for 12 months = ₹ 12, 000

		₹
∴	M/R for 8 months = $12000 \times \frac{8}{12}$	8,000
	Add: 50% of rent due for 4 months = (i.e. 4000 – 2000 or 50% of 4000) or $\left(12,000 \times \frac{4}{12} \times \frac{50}{100}\right)$	2,000
		10,000

Royalties Payable Chart

Year	Royalty	Minimum rent	Short workings	Surplus	Short workings Recovered	Short workings Not recovered	Amt. payable to landlord
	₹	₹	₹	₹	₹	₹	₹
2006-07	7,000	12,000	5,000	-	-	-	12,000
2007-08	10,200	12,000	1,800	-	-	-	12,000
2008-09	19,000	12,000	-	7,000	2,500	-	16,500
Strike **2009-10**	10,800	9,600	-	1,200	1,200	1,300	9,600
Lock-out 2010-11	9,000	10,000	1,000	-	-	1,800	10,000

Minimum Rent A/c

Dr. Cr.

		₹			₹
2007 Mar. 31	To landlord's A/c	12,000	2007 Mar. 31	By royalties A/c	7,000
				By short-workings A/c	5,000
		12,000			12,000
2008 Mar. 31	To landlord's A/c	12,000	2008 Mar. 31	By royalties A/c	10,200
				By short-workings	1,800
		12,000			12,000
2011 Mar. 31	To landlord's A/c	10,000	2011 Mar. 31	By royalties A/c	9,000
				By short-workings	1,000
		10,000			10,000

Landlord's A/c

Dr. Cr.

		₹			₹
2007 Mar. 31	To cash A/c	12,000	2007 Mar. 31	By minimum rent A/c	12,000
		12,000			12,000

(Contd.)

(Contd.)

2008			2008		
Mar. 31	To cash A/c	12,000	Mar. 31	By minimum rent A/c	12,000
		12,000			12,000
2009			2009		
Mar. 31	To short-workings	2,500	Mar. 31	By royalties	19,000
	To cash A/c	16,500			
		19,000			19,000
2010			2010		
Mar. 31	To short-workings	1,200	Mar. 31	By royalties	10,800
	To cash A/c	9,600			
		10,800			10,800
2011			2011		
Mar. 31	To cash A/c	10,000	Mar. 31	By minimum rent A/c	10,000
		10,000			10,000

Royalties A/c

Dr. Cr.

		₹			₹
2007			2007		
Mar. 31	To minimum rent A/c	7,000	Mar. 31	By profit & loss A/c	7,000
		7,000			7,000
2008			2008		
Mar. 31	To minimum rent A/c	10,200	Mar. 31	By profit & loss A/c	10,200
		10,200			10,200
2009			2009		
Mar. 31	To landlord's A/c	19,000	Mar. 31	By profit & loss A/c	19,000
		19,000			19,000
2010			2010		
Mar. 31	To landlord's A/c	10,800	Mar. 31	By profit & loss A/c	10,800
		10,800			10,800
2011			2011		
Mar. 31	To minimum rent A/c	9,000	Mar. 31	By profit & loss A/c	9,000
		9,000			9,000

Short-workings A/c

Dr. Cr.

		₹			₹
2007			2007		
Mar. 31	To minimum rent A/c	5,000	Mar. 31	By balance c/d	5,000
		5,000			5,000
2008			2008		
Jan. 1	To balance B/d	5,000	Mar. 31	By balance c/d	6,800
Mar. 31	To minimum rent A/c	1,800			
		6,800			6,800
2009			2009		
Apr. 1	To balance B/d	6,800	Mar. 31	By landlord's A/c	2,500
				By balance c/d	4,300
		6,800			6,800
2010			2010		
Apr. 1	To balance B/d	4,300	Mar. 31	By landlord's A/c	1,200
				By profit & loss A/c	1,300
				By balance c/d	1,800
		4,300			4,300
2011			2011		
Apr. 1	To balance B/d	1,800	Mar. 31	By profit & loss A/c	1,800
Mar. 31	To minimum rent A/c	1,000		By balance c/d	1,000
		1,800			2,800
2012					
Apr. 1	To balance B/d	1,000			

Illustration 11: (Without minimum rent A/c)

Mr. Chandra wrote a textbook on Business Management and got it published through Veda Book House on 1.1.2007 on the following terms:

He was to receive royalty of Rs. 10 per copy sold subject to a minimum rent of Rs. 50,000 p.a. allowing the Veda Book House to recover any short-workings during the first 4 years. Other details were:

Year	No. of copies printed	Closing stock
2007	3,000	1,000
2008	4,000	2,000
2009	8,000	3,000
2010	5,000	1,500
2011	6,000	500

Pass Journal entries in the books of Veda Book House for five years.

(B.U. Non-semester scheme April 2000)

Solution:

Working Notes:

(1) Royalty is based on the number of copies sold, but information regarding copies sold is not given in the problem. Hence, to start with, let us ascertain the number of copies sold as follows:

Year	No. of copies sold	=	Opening stock	+	No. of copies printed	–	Closing stock
2007	2,000	=	Nil	+	3,000	–	1,000
2008	3,000	=	1,000	+	4,000	–	2,000
2009	7,000	=	2,000	+	8,000	–	3,000
2010	6,500	=	3,000	+	5,000	–	1,500
2011	7,000	=	1,500	+	6,000	–	500

Royalties payable chart

Year	No. of copies sold	Royalty Rs 10 copy	Minimum Rent	Short-Workings	Surplus	Short-workings		Amt. payable to landlord
						Recovered	Not Recovered	
		₹	₹	₹	₹	₹	₹	₹
2007	2,000	20,000	50,000	30,000	-	-	-	50,000
2008	3,000	30,000	50,000	20,000	-	-	-	50,000
2009	7,000	70,000	50,000	-	20,000	20,000	-	50,000
2010	6,500	65,000	50,000	-	15,000	15,000	15,000	50,000
2011	7,000	70,000	50,000	-	20,000	-	-	70,000

Journal entries in the books of Veda Book House

Date	Particulars		L.F.	Dr. ₹	Cr. ₹
2007					
Dec. 31	Royalties A/c	Dr.		20,000	
	Short-workings A/c	Dr.		30,000	
	To Chandra's A/c				50,000
	(Being M/R payable)				

(Contd.)

(Contd.)

Dec. 31	Chandra's A/c Dr.		50,000	
	To Cash A/c			50,000
	(Being M/R paid)			
Dec. 31	Profit and loss A/c Dr.		20,000	
	To royalties A/c			20,000
	(Being royalties transferred)			
2008				
Dec. 31	Royalties A/c Dr.		30,000	
	Short-workings A/c Dr.		20,000	
	To Chandra's A/c			50,000
	(Being M/R payable)			
Dec. 31	Chandra's A/c Dr.		50,000	
	To cash A/c			50,000
	(Being M/R paid)			
Dec. 31	Profit and loss A/c Dr.		30,000	
	To Royalties A/c			30,000
	(Being royalties transferred)			
2009				
Dec. 31	Royalties A/c Dr.		70,000	
	To Chandra's A/c			70,000
	(Being royalties payable)			
Dec. 31	Chandra's A/c Dr.		70,000	
	To short-workings A/c			20,000
	To cash A/c			50,000
	(Being part of S/W recovered and balance is paid)			
Dec. 31	Profit and loss A/c Dr.		70,000	
	Royalties A/c			70,000
	(Being royalties transferred)			
2010				
Dec. 31	Royalties A/c Dr.		65,000	
	To Chandra's A/c			65,000
	(Being royalties payable)			
Dec. 31	Chandra's A/c Dr.		65,000	
	To short-workings A/c			15,000
	To cash A/c			50,000
	(Being part of S/W recovered & balance is paid)			
Dec. 31	Profit and loss A/c Dr.		80,000	
	To royalties A/c			65,000
	To short-workings A/c			15,000

(Contd.)

(Contd.)

	(Being transfer of royalties and irrecoverable short-workings)			
2011				
Dec. 31	Royalties A/c Dr.		70,000	
	To Chandra's A/c			70,000
	(Being royalties payable)			
Dec. 31	Chandra's A/c Dr.		70,000	
	To Cash A/c			70,000
	(Being royalties paid)			
Dec. 31	Profit and Loss A/c Dr.		70,000	
	To Royalties A/c			70,000
	(Being royalties transferred)			

4.8 ACCOUNTING PROCEDURE IN THE BOOKS OF LANDLORD

(1) For Royalties receivable:
Lessee's A/c Dr.
To Royalties Receivable A/c.

(2) If there is short-workings = Lessee's A/c Dr
To Royalties Receivable A/c
To Short-workings allowable A/c

(3) If there is no recoupment of short-workings = Cash A/c
To Lessee's A/c

(4) If Short-working are recovered by Tenant: Cash A/c Dr.
Short-working A/c Dr.
To Lessee's A/c

(5) For transfer of Royalties Receivable:- Royalties Receivable A/c Dr
To Profit and Loss A/c

(6) For irrecoverable short-workings (if any):
Short-workings (irrecovered) Dr.
To profit and loss

4.9 PROBLEMS AND SOLUTIONS

Illustration 12: (Strike Period – Actual royalty discharges all rental obligations)

Ajantha coal company took property from Bharath Ltd on lease at a royalty of ₹ 5 per ton of coal raised with a minimum rent of ₹ 50,000 per annum. Each years minimum rent over royalties is recoverable out of royalties of next two years only. In the event of strike if the minimum rent is not reached the lease provided that the actual royalties earned for that year shall discharge all the rental obligations.

The output of coal was as follows:

Year	Output
2007	7,000 tons
2008	11,000 tons
2009	11,500 tons
2010	9,000 tons
2011	8,000 tons (Strike year)

Pass necessary journal entries in the books of Bharath Ltd. (landlord) and also prepary necessary ledger A/cs.

(Gulbarga University 1996 – adapted)

Solution:

Royalties Payable Chart

Year	Output (ton)	Royalty ₹ 5 per ton	Minimum rent	Short Workings	Surplus	Short workings Recovered	Short workings Not recovered	Amt. payable to landlord
	₹	₹	₹	₹	₹	₹	₹	₹
2007	7,000	35,000	50,000	15,000	-	-	-	50,000
2008	11,000	55,000	50,000	-	5,000	5,000	-	50,000
2009	11,500	57,500	50,000	-	7,500	7,500	2,500	50,000
2010	9,000	45,000	50,000	5,000	-	-	-	50,000
Strike 2011	8,000	40,000	50,000	-	-	-	-	40,000

In the books of Bharath Ltd. (Landlord)

Date	Particulars	L.F.	Dr. ₹	Cr. ₹
2007 Dec. 31	Ajantha Ltd. A/c Dr. To Royalties Receivable A/c To Short-workings Allowable A/c (Being Minimum Rent receivable)		50,000	 25,000 15,000

(Contd.)

(Contd.)

Dec. 31	Cash / Bank A/c Dr.		50,000	
	To Ajantha Ltd A/c			50,000
	(Being minimum rent received)			
Dec. 31	Royalties receivable A/c Dr.		35,000	
	To profit and loss A/c			35,000
	(Being transfer of royalties receivable)			
2008				
Dec. 31	Ajantha Ltd., A/c Dr.		55,000	
	To royalties receivable A/c			55,000
	(Being royalties receivable)			
Dec. 31	Cash / bank A/c Dr.		50,000	
	Short workings allowable A/c Dr.		5,000	
	To Ajantha Ltd., A/c			55,000
	(Being tenant is allowed to recover part of S/W and balance is received)			
Dec. 31	Royalties receivable A/c Dr.		55,000	
	To profit and loss A/c			55,000
	(Being transfer & royalties receivable)			
2009				
Dec. 31	Ajantha Ltd., A/c Dr.		57,500	
	To royalties receivable A/c			57,500
	(Being royalties receivable)			
Dec. 31	Cash A/c Dr.		50,000	
	Short workings allowable A/c		7,500	
	To Ajantha Ltd. A/c			57,500
	(Being tenant is allowed to recover part of the S/W and balance is received)			
Dec. 31	Short-workings allowable A/c		2,500	
	Royalties receivable A/c Dr.		57,500	
	To profit and loss A/c			60,000
	(Being S/W not recovered by Tenant and royalties reeivable transfered)			
2010				
Dec. 31	Ajantha Ltd., A/c		50,000	
	To royalties receivable A/c			45,000
	To short-workings allowable A/c			5,000
	(Being M/R receivable)			
Dec. 31	Cash A/c Dr.		50,000	
	To Ajantha Ltd., A/c			50,000
	(Being M/R received)			

(Contd.)

(Contd.)

Dec. 31	Royalties receivable A/c Dr.		45,000	
	To profit and loss A/c			45,000
	(Being transfer of royalties receivable)			
2011				
Dec. 31	Ajantha Ltd., A/c Dr.		40,000	
	To royalties receivable A/c			40,000
	(Being actual royalty earned receivable during strike period)			
Dec. 31	Cash A/c Dr.		40,000	
	To Ajantha Ltd., A/c			40,000
	(Being royalties received)			
Dec. 31	Royalties receivable A/c Dr.		40,000	
	To profit & loss A/c			40,000
	(Being transfer of royalties receivable)			

Ledger accounts in the books of Bharath Ltd. (Landlord)

Royalties receivable A/c

Dr. Cr.

	₹		₹
2007		2007	
Dec. 31 To Profit and Loss A/c	35,000	Dec. 31 By Ajantha Ltd.	35,000
	35,000		35,000
2008		2008	
Dec. 31 To Profit and Loss A/c	55,000	Dec. 31 By Ajantha Ltd.	55,000
	55,000		55,000
2009		2009	
Dec. 31 To Profit and Loss A/c	57,500	Dec. 31 By Ajantha Ltd.	57,500
	57,500		57,500
2010		2010	
Dec. 31 To Profit and Loss A/c	45,000	Dec. 31 By Ajantha Ltd.	45,000
	45,000		45,000
2011		2011	
Dec. 31 To Profit and Loss A/c	40,000	Dec. 31 By Ajantha Ltd.	40,000
	40,000		40,000

Ajantha Limited A/c (Lessee's A/c)

Dr. Cr.

		₹			₹
2007			2007		
Dec. 31	To royalties receivable A/c	35,000	Dec. 31	By cash/bank A/c	50,000
	To short-workings allowable A/c	15,000			
		50,000			50,000
2008			2008		
Dec. 31	Royalties receivable A/c	55,000	Dec. 31	By cash/bank A/c	50,000
				By short-workings allowable A/c	5,000
		55,000			55,000
2009			2009		
Dec. 31	Royalties receivable A/c	57,500	Dec. 31	By cash/bank A/c	50,000
				By short workings allowable A/c	7,500
		57,500			57,500
2010			2010		
Dec. 31	Royalties receivable A/c	45,000	Dec. 31	By cash/bank A/c	50,000
	To short-workings allowable A/c	5,000			
		50,000			50,000
2011			2011		
Dec. 31	Royalties receivable	40,000	Dec. 31	By cash/bank A/c	40,000
		40,000			40,000

Short-workings allowable A/c

Dr. Cr.

		₹			₹
2007			2007		
Dec. 31	To balance c/d	15,000	Dec. 31	By Ajantha Ltd.	15,000
		15,000			15,000
2008			2008		
Dec. 31	To Ajantha Ltd.	5,000	Jan. 1	By balance B/d	15,000
	To Balance c/d	10,000			
		15,000			15,000

(Contd.)

(Contd.)

2009			2009		
Dec. 31	Ajantha Ltd	7,500	Jan. 1	By balance B/d	10,000
	To Profit and Loss A/c	2,500			
		10,000			10,000
2010			2010		
Dec. 31	To Ajantha Ltd	5,000	Dec. 31	By balance c/d	5,000
		5,000			5,000
2011			2011		
Dec. 31	To balance c/d	5,000	Dec. 31	By balance B/d	5,000
		5,000			5,000
			2012		
			Jan. 1	By balance B/d	5,000

Illustration 13: (Ledger A/cs in the books of Landlord / Lesser)

Mr. Ramanujam patented an automatic door closer and granted to Mr. Raju the licence to manufacture and sell the closers for 10 years on the following terms:

(a) Raju to pay a royalty of ₹ 5 for every closer sold with a Minimum rent of ₹ 2,500 p.a.

(b) Raju could set-off short workings arising in any year against surplus royalties payable in the next 2 years.

(c) From the second year onwards the dead rent is agreed upon at ₹ 2,000 instead of ₹ 2,500 and all other terms being unchanged.

The other details were:

Year	Productions (units)	Closing stock (units)
2008	125	25
2009	225	50
2010	285	35
2011	515	50

Show necessary ledger A/cs in the books of Mr. Ramanujam, the land lord.

(I. Sem. B.Com. B.U. Dec. 2006)

Solution:

Working Notes:

(1) Royalty is based on the number of door closers sold, which is not given in the problem. Hence, the same should be ascertained as follows:

No. of door closers sold = ?

Year	–	No. of closers sold	=	Opening stock	+	Production	–	Closing stock
2008	=	100	=	NIL	+	125	–	25
2009	=	200	=	25	+	225	–	50
2010	=	300	=	50	+	285	–	35
2011	=	500	=	35	+	515	–	50

Royalties Payable Chart

Year	No. of closers sold	Royalty ₹ 5	Minimum Rent	Short-workings	Surplus	Short-workings		Amt. payable to Landlord
						Recovered	Not recovered	
		₹	₹	₹	₹	₹	₹	
2008	100	500	2,500	2,000	-	-	-	2,5[illegible]00
2009	200	1,000	2,000	1,000	-	-	-	[illegible]00
2010	300	1500	2,000	500	-	-	2,000	2[illegible]00
2011	500	2,500	2,000	-	500	500	500	2[illegible]00

Royalties receivable A/c

Dr. Cr.

Date	Particulars	Amount	Date	Particulars	Amount
		₹			₹
2008			2008		
Dec. 31	To Profit and Loss A/c	500	Dec. 31	By Ramanujam A/c	[illegible]
		500			5[illegible]
2009			2009		
Dec. 31	To Profit and Loss A/c	1,000	Dec. 31	By Ramanujam A/c	1,[illegible]
		1,000			1[illegible]000
2010			2010		
Dec. 31	To Profit and Loss A/c	1,500	Dec. 31	By Ramanujam A/c	[illegible],500
		1,500			1[illegible]500

(Contd.)

(Contd.)

2011 Dec. 31	To Profit and Loss A/c	2,500	2011 Dec. 31	By Ramanujam A/c	2,500
		2,500			2,500

Mr. Raju's Account (Lessee)

Dr. Cr

		₹			₹
2008 Dec. 31	To royalties receivable A/c	500	2008 Dec. 31	By cash A/c	2,500
	To short-workings allowable A/c	2,000			
		2,500			2,500
2009 Dec. 31	To royalties receivable A/c	1,000	2009 Dec. 31	By cash A/c	2,000
	To short-workings allowable A/c	1,000			
		2,000			2,000
2010 Dec. 31	To royalties receivable A/c	1,500	2010 Dec. 31	By cash A/c	2,000
	To short-workings allowable A/c	500			
		2,000			2,000
2011 Dec. 31	To royalties A/c	2,500	2011 Dec. 31	By short-workings allowable A/c	500
				By cash A/c	2,000
		2,500			2,500

Short-workings A/c

Dr. Cr.

		₹			₹
2008 Dec. 31	To Balance C/d	2,000	2008 Dec. 31	By Raju's A/c	2,000
		2,000			2,000

(Contd.)

(Contd.)

2009 Dec. 31	To Balance C/d	3,000	2009 Jan 1 Dec. 31	By Balance B/d By Raju's A/c	2,000 1,000
		3,000			3,000
2010 Dec. 31	To Profit and Loss A/c To Balance c/d	2,000 1,500	2010 Jan. 1 Dec. 31	By Balance B/d By Raju's A/c	3,000 500
		3,500			3,500
2011 Dec. 31	To Raju's A/c To Profit and Loss A/c To Balance c/d	500 500 500	2011 Jan.1	By Balance B/d	1,500
		1,500			1,500
			2012 Jan. 1	By Balance b/d	500

4.10 EXERCISES

Section – A (2 marks)

1. What is royalty? (Nov 1998 & 2001)
2. Define royalty. (2004 June Sem. Scheme)
3. What do you mean by short-workings?
4. What is the entry for irrecoverable short-workings in the books of lesser? (B.U. I sem. B.Com Dec. 2004 / Dec. 2007)
5. Why is minimum rent clause included in the royalty agreement? (B.U. I Sem. B.Com Dec. 2005)
6. What is irrecoverable short-workings? (B.U I Sem. B.Com Dec. 2005)
7. Bring out the meaning of short-workings with an example. (B.U. I Sem. B.Com Nov. 2005)
8. How is irrecoverable short-workings A/c closed? (B.U. I Sem. B.Com Nov. 2007)
9. What do you mean by minimum rent? (B.U. I Sem. B.Com Dec. 2008)
10. Who is lessor?
11. Who is lessee?
12. What is meant by recoupment of short-workings?
13. What is surplus?
14. How do you treat irrecoverable short-workings in the books of a lessee?

15. How do you treat the effects of strike in royalty A/cs?
(B.U. I Sem. B.Com Nov. 2010)
16. What is short-workings? How do you treat it on the B/S of lessee of the recoupment period is over? (B.U. I Sem. B.com Nov. 2010)

Section – B (5 marks)

1. Prepare an analyzed table from the following details:
Royalty payable = 50 paise per ton of output
Minimum rent = Rs. 7,500 p.a.
Right of recoupment of short-workings = upto 3 years
Output during the first 3 years = 10,000, 14,000 and 18,000 tons respectively.
(BU. I Sem. B.Com Nov. 2004)
2. Prepare an analytical table of royalties from the following details:
(a) Minimum rent = ₹ 10,000 p.a.
(b) Royalty = ₹ 1 per tons of a/c raised.
(c) Short-workings are recoverable during the first 3 years of the lease only
(d) The output for first 4 years was:-
1990–2000 tons 1992–15000 tons and
1991–5000 tons 1993–2000 tons
(BU. I Sem. B.Com Nov. 2006)
3. Prepare short-workings A/c from the following details:
(a) Minimum rent – ₹ 2,000 p.a.
(b) Royalties payable = ₹ 5/- per ton.
(c) Short-workings can be recouped during first 4 years of lease only
(d) The production for the first 4 years were as follows:
2000 – 2,000 tons
2001 – 3,000 tons
2002 – 4,000 tons
2003 – 4,500 tons
4. Prepare an analytical table of royalties from the following details:
(1) Minimum rent = 2,30,000 p.a.
(2) Royalty = ₹ 2/- per ton of coal raised
(3) Short-workings are recoverable during the first 3 years of the lease only.
(4) The output for the first 4 years was:

Year	Output
2001	4,000 tons
2002	8,000 tons
2003	16,000 tons
2004	4,000 tons

(BU. I Sem. B.Com 2007)

5. Z Co. Ltd. took a lease from landlord for a period of 25 years from 1st, Jan. 2001 on a royalty of ₹ 2/- per ton of coal raised with a minimum rent of ₹ 20,000 and power to recoup short-workings during the first four years of the lease.
The annual output was as follows:
2001 = 500 tons, 2002 = 8,000 tons, 2003 = 10,000 tons,
2004 = 15,000 tons and 2005 = 20,000 tons
Prepare necessary journal entry in the books of 'Z' Company
(BU. I Sem. B.Com Nov. 2008)
6. A mining company leased a property from 'P' at a royalty of ₹ 5/- per ton with a minimum rent of Rs. 12,000 p.a. each year's excess of minimum rent over royalty is recoverable out by the royalties of next 3 years. The results of the workings are as follows:

Year	Output (tons)
2004	1,000
2005	1,500
2006	2,000
2007	2,800
2008	3,000

Prepare necessary ledger A/cs in the books by the company for 5 years.
(BU. I Sem. B.Com. Nov. 2009)
7. Nischal Mines Company took a lease from a landlord for a period of 10 years from 1st Jan, 2005 as a royalty of ₹ 10 per tons of coal raised with a dead rent of ₹ 40,000 p.a. and power of recoup short-workings during the first 4 years of the lease.
The annual output was as follows:

Year	Output (tons)
2005	2,000 tons
2006	3,000 tons
2007	4,000 tons
2008	4,500 tons
2009	5,000 tons

(Bu. I Sem. B.Com Nov. 2009)
8. Mr. Kiran, the author of accountancy book entered into royalty agreement with Bangalore Publishers Ltd. on 1-4-2005. The terms were a royalty of ₹ 50 per copy sold, be payable subject to a minimum rent of 4,00,000 p.a. with the right to recoup the short-workings during subsequent 2 years from the year on which short-workings arise. The other details:

Year		No. of copies printed		Closing stock
2005-06	-	6,200 copies	-	1,200 copies
2006-07	-	8,000 copies	-	1,800 copies
2007-08	-	9,000 copies	-	2,000 copies
2008-09	-	10,000 copies	-	1,500 copies
2009-10	-	12,000 copies	-	1,000 copies

(BU. B.Com. Nov. 2000)

9. Suresh leased a property from Ramesh at a royalty of ₹ 1 per ton with a minimum rent of ₹ 4,000 per annum on 1.1.2004. Lease provides that short-workings shall be recovered out of excess earning with first 5 years of the lease and in a period by strike the minimum rent stand reduced proportionately for the period out worked.
Working results were as follows:

Year =	2004	2005	2006	2007	2008	2009	2010
Production = (Tons)	Nil	1,300	3,700	4,500	7,000	2,400 (Strike for 6 months)	6,000

(BU. B.Com. Nov. 2002)

10. On 1st Jan 2004 'X' collieries leased some land from 'Y' for a minimum rent of Rs. 3,000 for 1st year, Rs, 5,000 for 2nd year and thereafter 10,000 p.a. merged into a royalty of 5 years per ton with power to recoup short-workings over 2 years after occurring short workings. The annual output for the first 4 years ending are:

2004	3,000 tons
2005	8,600 tons
2006	22,000 tons,
2007	18,000 tons (strike for 3 months)

There was a provison in the lease that on the extent of strike and minimum rent not being reached, the actual royalties earned for the year discharged all the rented obligations.

(B.U. B. Com. April 1988)

5

Conversion of a Partnership Firm into a Limited Company

SYNOPSIS

5.1 Introduction
5.2 Need or reasons for conversion
5.3 Purchase consideration – Meaning, methods and discharge.
5.4 Accounting procedure – Books of partnership firm.
5.5 Realisation A/c and revaluation A/c.
5.6 Accounting procedure – Books of purchasing company.
5.7 Problems and solutions – (Section – B) Type.
5.8 Problems and solutions – (Section – C) Type.
5.9 Excercizes.

5.1 INTRODUCTION

The partnership firm suffers from severe drawbacks such as: (1) unlimited liability, (2) limited capital, (3) lack of continuous existence, (4) lack of managerial skill or efficiency, (5) disputes among the partners etc. These drawbacks will not allow partnership firm to ensure earning profits or expansion of the business activities beyond certain level.

In order to overcome these drawbacks and enjoy the benefits of company form of business organisation, the partners of a firm may decide to convert the status partnership firm into a company, which is referred to as conversion of partnership into Company. This process of conversion results in dissolution of existing firm by means of selling its assets and liabilities to the company. The company formed for the purpose of taking over their business has to pay consideration to the partners.

5.2 NEED OR REASONS FOR / OBJECTIVES OF CONVERSION

The partners of a partnership firm may decide to convert their existing firm into a company or may sell their business to the existing company with a view to achieve the following:-

1. To enjoy the benefit of limited liability and the transferability of shares
2. To ensure perpetual existence
3. To increase the capital or financial strength of the business
4. To enjoy the opportunities for expansion of business
5. To enjoy the benefits of large scale production
6. To enjoy the status of separate legal entity
7. To enjoy the benefit of limited tax
8. To increase the managerial skills and ensure managerial efficiency.

5.3 PURCHASE CONSIDERATION – MEANING, METHODS AND DISCHARGE

Meaning

The purchase consideration is the purchase price payable by purchasing company to the partners (vendors) of the partnership firm for taking over their assets and liabilities.

The company may acquire the assets and liabilities, their book values or at market values, which depends upon the agreement entered into with partners. The purchase consideration so calculated may be paid in any form such as, shares and debentures, of the company and or in cash or partly in shares, partly in debentures and partly on cash.

Methods of Calculating Purchase Consideration

The purchase consideration may be calculated by adopting any one of the following methods:

(1) Lumpsum payment method
(2) Net assets method
(3) Net payments method.

1. Lumpsum Payment Method

Under this method, the entire purchase considerations agreed will be paid in one lumpsum say Rs. 1,00,000 i.e. fixed amount of consideration.

2. Net Assets Method

Under this method, purchase consideration is always equal to the difference between total agreed values of assets and liabilities taken over. For example, assets of a firm are taken over for ₹ 1,00,000 and liabilities for ₹ 30,000

∴ Purchase consideration is calculated as follows:

	₹
Total agreed value of assets taken over :	1,00,000
Less: Total agreed value of liabilities taken over :	30,000
∴ Purchase consideration	70,000

3. Net Payments Method

Under this method, purchase consideration is the sum total of all payments made by purchasing a company in the form of shares, debentures, and cash to the partnership firm.

5.4 ACCOUNTING PROCEDURE

In the Books of Partnership Firm (Vendors)

Closing Journal entries to wind up the affairs of partnership firm:

(1) For closing assets A/c:
Realisation A/c Dr.
To asset A/c (individually with book value)

(2) For closing liabilities A/c:
Liability A/c Dr. (Individually with book value)
To realisation A/c

(3) For the purchase consideration falling due:
Purchasing company A/c Dr.
To realisation A/c.

(4) For Assets (if any) taken over by partners:
Partners capital A/c Dr.
To Realisation A/c.

(5) For liabilities (if any) taken over by partners:
Realisation A/c Dr
To Partner's capital A/c.

(6) For Assets (if any) not taken over by purchasing company:
Cash/Bank A/c Dr.
To Realisation A/c.

(7) For liabilities (if any) not taken over by purchasing company:
Realisation A/c of
To cash/Bank

(8) For payment of realisation expenses or cost of winding up:
Realisation A/c Dr.
To cash/Bank

(9) For realisation expenses agreed to be paid by any partners:
Realisation expenses A/c Dr.
To Partner's capital A/c.

(10) For unrecorded liability (if any) were to be paid:
Realisation A/c Dr.
To cash A/c

(11) For closing Realisation A/c:
(a) When there is realisation profit:
Realisation A/c Dr.
To Partner's capital
(b) When there is realisation loss: Reverse entry.

(12) For closing partner's loan A/c (if any):
Partner's loan A/c Dr.
To cash A/c.

(13) For closing undistributed reserves or profits A/c:
RF/General reserve/P&L/Ac Dr.
To partner's capital A/c

(14) For closing undistributed losses (i.e.) fictious assets:
Partner's capital A/c Dr.
To profit & loss A/c

(15) For distribution of shares / Debentures of cash:
Partner's capital A/c Dr.
To Shares A/c.
To Debentures A/c.
To Cash

Note: In case of ratio distribution of shares / debentures entry is given in the problem, then, they should be distributed accordingly, otherwise, they should be distributed in final claim ratio.

Final claim ratio: Partner's capital + all credits – all debits = final claim, i.e., ratio of final claims of each partner.

5.5 REALISATION ACCOUNT

Realisation account is a temporary account prepared at the time of dissolution/ winding up of sole trading concern/partnership firm/joint stock company. It is a nominal account in nature. It is prepared to find out profit or loss on sale of assets and discharge of liabilities. It is closed by transferring realisation profit or loss to partner's capital A/cs.

Realisation A/c and Revalution A/c – Distinction

Points of difference	Realisation A/c	Revaluation A/c
1. Circumstances of preparation	– is prepared at the time of dissolution or winding up of the firm	– is prepared at the time of admission, retirement and death of a partner and also at the time of amalgamation of firms

(Contd.)

(Contd.)

2. Object of preparation	– is to ascertain profit or loss on sale of assets and discharge of liabilities.	– is to make adjustments in the values of assets and liabilities in the event of admissing retirement or death of partner.
3. Effect on entity of business	The activities of business will come to stand still and result in closure of business unit	Even after the preparation of the revaluation A/c., the firm continues to run its business

5.6 ACCOUNTING PROCEDURE IN THE BOOKS OF PURCHASING COMPANY

Opening entries/incorporation or acquistion entries:

(1) For purchase of business of firm:
Business purchase A/c Dr.
To vendor firm A/c.

(2) For incorporation of assets and liabilities taken over:
Assets A/c Dr (individually @ agreed values)
To liabilities (individually @ agreed values)
To Business purchase A/c.

(3) For final settlement of purchase consideration:
Vendor firm A/c Dr
To share capital A/c.
To debentures A/c.
To cash/bank A/c.

5.7 PROBLEMS AND SOLUTIONS (SECTION – B QUESTIONS)

Illustration 1: *(Net Payment Method)*

Calculate the amount of purchase consideration from the following details:
The purchasing company agreed to issue 15,000 equity shares of ₹ 10 each valued at ₹ 12 each. 6,000, 6% debentures of ₹ 10 each at a discount of 5%, pay cash equal to 10% of face value of shares and debentures issued. The company also agreed to meet dissolution expenses of ₹ 2,500.

(B.U. I Sem. B.Com. Dec. 2004)

Solution:

Calculation of purchase consideration:

(1) Issue of:	₹
(a) Equity shares: 15,000 shares × market price ₹ 12 =	1,80,000
(b) Debentures: 6,000, 6% Debs × Rs 10 – 5% discount	57,000

(2) Cash payment:

(a) Towards purchase consideration

= 15,000 shares × ₹ 10 =	1,50,000	
6,000 debs × ₹ 10 =	60,000	
	2,10,000	
∴ 10% of 2,10,000 the face value of (S) & (D)		21,000
(b) Towards dissolution expenses		2,500
		2,60,500

Illustration 2: Pass incorporation journal entries in the books of the company from the following particulars:

Purchase consideration = ₹ 2,50,000; value of sundry assets taken over = ₹ 3,00,000; current liabilities taken over = ₹ 30,000; settlement of purchase consideration = 60% in equity shares of ₹ 10 each at face value and the balance in 6% debentures of ₹ 100 each at face value.

(B.U. I Sem. B. Com., Dec. 2004)

Solution:

Incorporation journal entries in the books of company:

Date	Particulars	L.F.	Dr.	Cr.
1.	Business Purchase A/c Dr.		2,50,000	
	To M/s Vendor Firm A/c			2,50,000
	(Being Purchase of business of a firm)			
2.	Sundry Assets A/c Dr.		3,00,000	
	To Current liabilities A/c			30,000
	To Capital Reserve A/c			20,000
	To Business Purchase A/c			2,50,000
	(Being incorporation of assets & liabilities taken over)			
3.	M/s Vendor Firm A/c Dr.		2,50,000	
	To Equity Share Capital A/c			1,50,000
	To 6% Debentures A/c			1,00,000
	(Being discharge of P.C.)			

Illustration 3: *(Net Payments Method)*

Calculate the purchase consideration from the following details:

The purchasing company has agreed to issue:

(a) 8,000 equity shares of ₹ 10 each at pas,

(b) 500 8% preference shares of Rs 100 each at 10% premium.,

(c) 1,000 debentures of ₹ 50 each at 10% discount
(d) Pay cash equal to 10% of total purchase consideration.

(B.U. I. Sem. B. Com., Dec. 2005)

Solution:

		₹
1. Issue of:		
(a) 8,000 equity shares × Rs. 10 =		80,000
(b) 500, 8% pref. shares × Rs. 100 + 10% =		55,000
(c) 1,000 Debs × Rs. 50 – 10%		45,000
∴ 90% of P.C.		1,80,000
2. Cash payment = 10% of total P.C.:		
∴ 90% total P.C. = 1,80,000		
∴ 10% total P.C. = $\left(\frac{10}{90} \times 1,80,000\right)$		20,000
or $\left(1,80,000 \times \frac{100}{90} = 2,00,000\right)$	P.C.	2,00,000

Illustration 4: *(Net Assets Method)*

A company takes over the following assets and liabilities from a partnership firm:

	₹
Land and building	45,000
Plant and machinery	20,000
Stock	20,000
Debtors	23,200
Bills receivable	16,000
Current liabilities	28,800

The value of goodwill is fixed at 28,800, calculate purchase consideration, payable—10,000 equity shares of Rs. 10 each and balance in cash.

(B.U. I. Sem. B.com. Dec, 2009)

Solution 4:

(a) Calculation of purchase consideration:

Assets taken over:	₹
Goodwill	28,800
Land and buildings	45,000
Plant and machinery	20,000
Stock	20,000
Debtors	23,200
Bills receivable	16,000
Total agreed value of assets taken over	1,53,000

Less: Total agreed value of liabilities taken over Current liabilities	28,800
Purchase consideration	1,24,200

(b) Mode of payment of purchase consideration

(i) in equity shares = 10,000 equity shares × Rs. 10 =	1,00,000
(ii) in cash (balance)	24,200
∴ Purchase consideration	1,24,200

5.8 PROBLEMS AND SOLUTIONS (SECTION – C QUESTION)

A. Lump Sum Payment Method

Illustration 5: Rocket, Pocket and Jocket were partners sharing profits and losses equally. They decided to sell their firm to Secret Co. Ltd., on 31.12.2011 on which date their balance sheet stood as follows:

Capital liabilities	Amt. (₹)	Assets	Amt. (₹)
Capital A/cs : Rocket	5,40,000	Plant and machinery	3,42,000
Pocket	3,60,000	Stock	3,00,000
Jocket	1,80,000	Sundry debtors	2,70,000
Sundry creditors	1,02,000	Cash	1,80,000
		Profit and loss A/c	90,000
	11,82,000		11,82,000

Secret Company Ltd., a new company was registered with an authorized capital of Rs. 10,00,000 consisting of shares of Rs. 100 each, for the purpose of taking over business of the above partnership firm. The purchase price of the firm was agreed to Rs. 9,87,000. The company paid the purchase price by the issue of 9,000 fully paid shares and the balance in cash. The cost of winding up amounted to Rs. 15,000. Assuming that shares received are distributed in the capital ratio of partners, Pass the necessary Journal entries to close the books of the firm. Also prepare the ledger A/cs necessary.

Solution:

Working Notes

(1) Purchase consideration is fixed at Rs. 9,87,000.

(2) Purchase consideration is payable as to:
Rs. 9,00,000 in shares of Rs. 100 each and the balance of Rs. 87,000 in cash.

(3) Shares are distributed in capital ratio of partners:
i.e., 5,40,000 3,60,000; 1,80,000 or 3:2:1 ratio.

Journal entries to close the books of partnership firm.

	Particulars		Dr.	Cr.
1.	Realisation A/c	Dr.	10,92,000	
	To plant and machinery A/c			3,42,000
	To stocks A/c			3,00,000
	To sundry debtors A/c			2,70,000
	To cash A/c			1,80,000
	(Being assets accounts closed)			
2.	Sundry creditors	Dr.	1,02,000	
	To Realisation A/c			1,02,000
	(Being liabilities a/c closed)			
3.	Secret company account	Dr.	9,87,000	
	To Realisation A/c			9,87,000
	(Being purchase consideration falling due)			
4.	Shares in secret company A/c	Dr.	9,00,000	
	Cash A/c	Dr.	87,000	
	To Realisation A/c			9,87,000
	(Being purchase consideration received)			
5.	Realisation A/c	Dr.	15,000	
	To cash A/c			15,000
	(Being winding-up cost net)			
6.	Rocket's capital A/c	Dr.	6,000	
	Pocket's capital A/c	Dr.	6,000	
	Jocket's capital A/c	Dr.	6,000	
	To realisation A/c			18,000
	(Being transfer of realisation loss in their respective profit sharing ratio)			
7.	Rocket's capital A/c	Dr.	30,000	
	Pocket's capital A/c	Dr.	30,000	
	Jocket's capital A/c	Dr.	30,000	
	To profit and loss A/c			90,000
	(Being transfer of undistributed loss)			
8.	Rocket's capital A/c	Dr.	4,50,000	
	Pocket's capital A/c	Dr.	3,00,000	
	Jocket's capital A/c	Dr.	1,50,000	
	To shares in secret company A/c			9,00,000
	(Being distribution of shares received from purchasing co. in capital ratio 3:2:1)			
9.	Cash A/c	Dr.	6,000	
	To Jocket's capital A/c			6,000
	(Being deficit capital brought in cash)			
10.	Rocket's capital A/c	Dr.	54,000	
	Pocket's capital A/c	Dr.	24,000	
	To cash A/c			78,000
	(Being excess capital of partners paid in cash)			

Ledger A/cs on the books of firm

Dr. Realisation A/c Cr.

Particulars	₹	Particulars	₹
To plant and machinery A/c	3,42,000	By sundry creditors A/c	1,02,000
To stock A/c	3,00,000	To secret company A/c	9,87,000
To sundry debtors A/c	2,70,000	To loss transferred to:	
To cash A/c	1,80,000	Rocket's capital 1/3 6,000	
To cash A/c (cost of winding)	15,000	Pocket's capital 1/3 6,000	
		Jocket's capital 1/3 6,000	18,000
	11,07,000		11,07,000

Dr. Partners' Capital Account Cr.

Particulars	Rocket ₹	Pocket ₹	Jocket ₹	Particulars	Rocket ₹	Pocket ₹	Jocket ₹
To realisation A/c (loss)	6,000	6,000	6,000	By balance B/d	5,40,000	3,60,000	1,80,000
To profit & loss A/c – loss	30,000	30,000	30,000	By cash A/c	-	-	6,000
To shares in Secret Co. A/c	4,50,000	3,00,000	1,50,000				
To Cash A/c	54,000	24,000	-				
	5,40,000	3,60,000	1,86,000		5,40,000	3,60,000	1,86,000

Dr. Cash Account Cr.

Particulars	₹	Particulars	₹
To Secret Co. A/c	87,000	By realisation A/c – exps	15,000
To Jocket's capital A/c	6,000	By Rocket's capital A/c	54,000
		By Pocket's capital A/c	24,000
	93,000		93,000

Secret Company A/c
(Purchasing company A/c)

Dr. Cr.

Particulars	₹	Particulars	₹
To Realisation A/c	9,87,000	By shares in Secret Co. A/c	9,00,000
		By cash A/c	87,000
	9,87,000		9,87,000

Shares in Secret Company A/c

	₹		₹
To Secret Co. A/c	9,00,000	By Rocket's capital 3/6 By Pocket's capital 2/6 By Jocket's capital A/c 1/6	4,50,000 3,00,000 1,50,000
	9,00,000		9,00,000

Illustration 6: *(Lump Sum Payment Method)*
Jaya and Vijaya were partners sharing profits and losses in ratio of 2:1 respectively agreed to convert their firm into a Ltd. company on 31st Dec. 2011, on which date their balance sheet was as follows:

Liabilities	₹	Assets	₹
Sundry creditors	90,000	Cash	21,000
Mortgage on freehold property	30,000	Debtors	78,000
Capitals: Jaya	60,000	Stocks	48,000
Vijaya	30,000	Free hold property	48,000
		Plant	15,000
	2,10,000		2,10,000

The Ltd. company took all assets and liabilities with exception of mortgage on property for Rs. 1,80,000 payable as to Rs. 36,000 in cash, Rs. 72,000 in debentures and the balance on equity shares.

Close the books of the firm by preparing necessary ledger accounts assuming that partner's agree to share debentures and shares in proportion to their capital's given in the balance sheet.

Solution:

Working Notes:

(1) The purchase consideration is fixed at ₹ 1,80,000.

(2) Mode of payment of purchase consideration:

		₹
(a)	In shares (Balance)	72,000
(b)	In debentures and	72,000
(c)	In cash	36,000
		1,80,000

(3) Shares and debentures received as a part of purchase consideration has to be distributed in ratio of capitals disclosed in B/S i.e., 60,000; 30,000 or 2:1 ratio.

Ledger accounts to close the books of A/c Jaya & Vijaya firm

Dr. Realisation A/c Cr.

Particulars	₹	Particulars	₹
To cash A/c	21,000	By sundry creditors A/c	90,000
To sundry debtors A/c	78,000	By mortgage on freehold property	30,000
To stock A/c	48,000	By Ltd., company A/c	1,80,000
To freehold property A/c	48,000		
To plant A/c	15,000		
To cash – Mortgage on property A/c	30,000		
To profit transferred to: Jaya's capital 40,000 Vijaya's capital 20,000	60,000		
	3,00,000		3,00,000

Dr. Limited Company A/c (Purchasing company A/c) Cr.

Particulars	₹	Particulars	₹
To realisation A/c	1,80,000	By shares in Ltd. co. A/c	72,000
		By debentures in Ltd. co. A/c	72,000
		By cash A/c	36,000
	1,80,000		1,80,000

Dr. Capital A/cs of partners Cr.

Particulars	Jaya ₹	Vijaya ₹	Particulars	Jaya ₹	Vijaya ₹
To shares in Ltd. co. A/c (2:1)	48,000	24,000	By balance B/d	60,000	30,000
To debentures in Ltd. co. (2:1)	48,000	24,000	By Realisation A/c (profit)	40,000	20,000
To cash A/c (balance)	4,000	2,000			
	1,00,000	50,000		1,00,000	50,000

Dr. Cash A/c Cr.

	₹		₹
To Ltd. company A/c	36,000	By Realisation A/c (Mortgage loan) By Jaya's capital A/c By Vijaya's capital A/c	 30,000 4,000 2,000
	36,000		36,000

Dr. Shares in Ltd. co. A/c Cr.

	₹		₹
To Ltd. co. A/c	72,000	By Jaya's capital A/c By Vijaya's capital A/c	48,000 24,000
	72,000		72,000

Dr. Debentures in Ltd. co. A/c Cr.

	₹		₹
To Ltd. co. A/c	72,000	By Jaya's capital A/c By Vijaya's capital A/c	48,000 24,000
	72,000		72,000

B. Problems on Net Assets Method

Illustration 7:

Anand and Bhushan carrying on business in partnership resolved to dissolve the firm and set-off the business to "C" Co. Ltd., on 31st Dec, 2011, when their position was as under:

Balance sheet

Liabilities	₹	Assets	₹
Capitals: Anand Bhushan Sundry creditors	34,000 17,000 21,250	Land Furniture Stocks Debtors Cash	40,000 3,320 15,380 8,430 5,120
	72,250		72,250

The arrangement with the company was as follows:

(a) Land purchased at Rs. 50,000.
(b) Furniture and stock are taken at 10% below the book value.
(c) Goodwill of the firm is valued at Rs. 7,500.
(d) Debtors are taken at 8,000. But the creditors at the Balance Sheet figure.
(e) The purchase consideration is to be discharged by the company in fully paid equity shares of Rs. 10 each.

Pass the necessary Journal entries to close the books of the firm and also prepare ledger accounts necessary.

(B.U. April 1991)

Solution:

Working Notes:

(1) First, we have to calculate purchase consideration adopting suitable method. In this case, information regarding values at which assets and liabilities are taken over is given. Hence, purchase considerations has to be calculated adopting 'Net Assets Method' as under:-

Calculation of purchase consideration

Assets taken-over:	₹
Goodwill	7,500
Land	50,000
Furniture (Book value – 10%)	2,988
Stock (Book value – 10%)	13,842
Debtors	8,000
Total agreed value assets taken over	82,330
Less: Total agreed value of liabilities takenover: Sy. creditors	21,250
∴ Purchase consideration	61,080

(2) In this problem, it is not specifically stated as to whether the cash is taken over by purchasing company or not. Hence, the student has a choice to make his own assumption and work out the problem accordingly. As such, it is assumed that cash is not taken over.

(3) Cash is a liquid asset and therefore, cannot be realised. Hence, cash is not transfered to realisting a/c cash a/c can be closed by distributing the same among partners ultimately.

(4) In this problem, the profit sharing ratio is not given. Hence, it should be asumed that they are equal partners.

Journal entries to close the books of Anand and Bhushan firm

Date	Particulars		L.F.	Dr.	Cr.
				₹	₹
2011					
Dec. 31	1. Realisation A/c	Dr.		67,130	
	To land A/c				40,000
	To furniture A/c				3,320
	To stock A/c				15,380
	To Sy. debtors A/c				8,430
	(Being asset accounts closed)				
	2. Sy. creditors A/c	Dr.		21,250	
	To realisation A/c				21,250
	(Being creditors a/c closed)				
	3. 'C' Co. Ltd. A/c (Purchasing co. A/c)	Dr.		61,080	
	To realisation A/c	Dr.			61,080
	(Being P.C. falling due)				
	4. Realisation A/c	Dr.		15,200	
	To Anand's capital A/c				7,600
	To Bhushan's capital A/c				7,600
	(Being transfer of realisation Profit in profit sharing ratio)				
	5. Anand's capital A/c	Dr.		38,380	
	Bhushan's capital A/c	Dr.		22,700	
	To shares in 'C' Co. Ltd. A/c				61,080
	(Being shares received from Purchasing company are distributed in final claim ratio of 208:123)				
	6. Anand's capital A/c	Dr.		3,220	
	Bhushan's capital A/c	Dr.		1,900	
	To Cash A/c				5,120
	(Being remaining balance due to partners is settled by the payment of cash)				

Working Note 5

As no agreed ratio is given in the problem for distribution of share received from C. Co. Ltd., shares therefore, are to be distributed in final claim ratio.

Final claim ratio is the ratio of final amount due to partners on the completion of dissolution process. Which is ascertained as follows:

	Anand	Bhushan
	₹	₹
Capital as per B/S given	34,000	17,000
Add: Realisation profit	7,600	7,600
∴ Finally amount due to partner	41,600	24,600
∴ Ratio of final claim	416 :	246
or	208 :	123

∴ Shares are distributed in the ratio of 208 : 123 converting if any fraction to record figure Say,

$$\text{Anand} = \frac{208}{331} \times 61,080 \qquad \text{Bhushan} = \frac{123}{331} \times 61080$$

$$= 38,380 \qquad\qquad = 22,700$$

Ledger accounts to close the books of firm

Realisation A/c

Dr. Cr.

	₹		₹
To land A/c	40,000	By sy. creditors A/c	21,250
To furniture A/c	3,320	By C. Co. Ltd A/c	61,080
To stock A/c	15,380	(Purchasing co.)	
To Sy. debtors A/c	8,430		
To profit transferred to:-			
Anand's capital A/c 7,600			
Bhushan's capital A/c 7,600	15,200		
	82,330		82,330

C. Co. Ltd. A/c (Purchasing Co.)

Dr. Cr.

	₹		₹
To realisation A/c	61,080	By Shares in 'C' Co. Ltd. A/c	61,080
	61,080		61,080

Dr. Capital A/cs of Partners Cr.

Particulars	Anand ₹	Bhushan ₹	Particulars	Anand ₹	Bhushan ₹
To shares in 'C' Co. Ltd. A/c	38,380	22,700	By balance B/d	34,000	17,000
To cash A/c (Bal. by)	3,220	1,900	By realisation A/c (Profit)	7,600	7,600
	41,600	34,600		41,600	34,600

Dr. Cash A/c Cr.

	₹		₹
To Balance B/d	5,120	By Anand's capital	3,220
		By Bhushan's capital	1,900
	5,120		5,120

Dr. Shares in 'C' co. Ltd/ A/c Cr.

	₹		₹
To 'C' Co. Ltd. A/c	61,080	By Anand's capital A/c	38,380
		By Bhushan's capital A/c	22,700
	61,080		61,080

Illustration 8:

David and Eshwar sharing profits and losses equally decided to convert their business into a Ltd. company on 31st Dec 2011, when their balance sheet stood as follows:

Liabilities	₹	Assets	₹
Sy. creditors	24,000	Cash balance	33,000
Loan creditors	20,000	Sy. debtors	7,000
Bank overdraft	8,000	Bills receivable	5,000
Reserve fund	3,000	Stock	8,000
Capitals: David	20,000	Patents	4,000
Eshwar	20,000	Machinery	8,000
		Land and building	30,000
	95,000		95,000

The company has agreed to base the purchase consideration on the following:

(a) The Goodwill of the firm will be valued at 2 years purchase of average profits of the previous 3 years. Profit in 2008 – Rs. 18,000, 2009 to Rs. 21,000 and in 2010 – Rs. 21,000.

(b) The company will take over the loan creditors by offering 9% preference shares, the company will not take over sundry creditors and the overdraft.

(c) Land and buildings will be valued at Rs. 50,000 and machinery at 12,000 and all other assets taken (except cash) are valued at their book values.

(d) The vendor to be allotted ordinary shares of Rs. 10 each to the amount equivalent to purchase consideration.

You are required to show:

(i) Realisation A/c and capital A/cs of partners in the books of firm

(ii) Opening journal entries in the books of purchasing company and also prepare the opening balance sheet.

(B.U. April 1986, October 1991, Oct 1998, Oct 2001)

Solution:

Working Notes:

(1) It is specifically stated that the purchasing co. will pay for goodwill of firm, which is calculated as under:

(i) Total Profit:

Year	Profit
2008	18,000
2009	21,000
2010	21,000
Total profit for 3 yrs.	60,000

(ii) Average Profit = Total profit ÷ 3 yrs.

60,000 ÷ 3 yrs.

Average profit = 20,000

(iii) Goodwill : Average profit × 2 years purchase

∴ 20,000 × 2

Goodwill = ₹ 40,000

(2) It is also stated clearly that purchasing company takes over only loan creditors. Hence, creditors and bank overdraft must be discharged by the firm itself.

(3) It is stated that land and buildings and machinery are taken over at agreed values of Rs. 50,000 and 12,000 respectively and other assets at their book value excluding cash balance.

(4) Calculation of purchase consideration:

Assets taken over :	₹
Goodwill	40,000
Land and building	50,000
Machinery	12,000
Debtors	7,000
B/R	5,000
Stock	8,000
Patents	4,000
∴ Total agreed value of assets taken over	1,26,000
Less: Total agreed value of liabilities taken over – loan creditors	20,000
∴ Purchase consideration	1,06,000

(5) Mode of payment of purchase consideration:
The entire purchase consideration is paid by the issue of ordinary shares of Rs. 10 each.
∴ 10,600 ordinary shares of Rs. 10 are issued towards purchase consideration.

Ledger accounts in the books of firm (David and Eshwar)

Dr. Realisation A/c Cr.

	₹		₹
To land and building A/c	30,000	By loan creditor A/c	20,000
To machinery A/c	8,000	By sy. creditors A/c	24,000
To sy. debtors A/c	7,000	By bank overdraft A/c	8,000
To bills receivable A/c	5,000	By limited company A/c	1,06,000
To stock A/c	8,000	(Purchasing co.)	
To patents A/c	4,000		
To cash A/c – (?? + old)	32,000		
To profit transferred to:			
David 1/2 – 32,000			
Eshwar 1/2 – 32,000	64,000		

Dr. Capital A/cs of partners Cr

Particulars	David ₹	Eshwar ₹	Particulars	David ₹	Eshwar ₹
To shares in Ltd. Co. 1:1	53,000	53,000	By balance B/d	20,000	20,000
To cash A/c	500	500	By realisation A/c profit	32,000	32,000
			By reserve fund 1:1	1,500	1,500
	53,500	53,500		53,500	53,500

Dr. Cash A/c Cr.

	₹		₹
To balance B/d	33,000	By Realisation A/c: Crs 24,000 o/d 8,000	32,000
		By David's capital A/c	500
		By Eshwar's capital A/c	500
	33,000		33,000

Dr. Limited company A/c (Purchasing Co.) Cr.

	₹		₹
To Realisation A/c	1,06,000	By ordinary shares in Ltd. Co. A/c	1,06,000
	1,06,000		1,06,000

Dr. Shares in Ltd., Co. A/c Cr.

	₹		₹
To Limited Company A/c	1,06,000	By David's capital A/c	53,000
		By Eshwar's capital A/c	53,000
	1,06,000		1,06,000

Opening or incorporation entries in the books of purchasing company

	Particulars		Dr. ₹	Cr. ₹
1.	Business Purchase A/c	Dr.	1,06,000	
	To Vendor Firm A/c			1,06,000
	(Being Purchase of business belonging to David and Eshwar's Firm)			
2.	Goodwill A/c	Dr.	40,000	
	Land and building	Dr.	50,000	
	Machinery A/c	Dr.	12,000	
	Bills receivable A/c	Dr.	5,000	
	Stock A/c	Dr.	8,000	

(Contd.)

(Contd.)

	Patents A/c	Dr.	4,000	
	Sy. Debtors A/c		7,000	
	To loan creditors A/c			20,000
	To business purchase A/c			1,06,000
	(Being incorporation of assets and liabilities taken over)			
3.	Loan creditor A/c	Dr.	20,000	
	To 9% preference share capital A/c			20,000
	(Being discharge of loan as by the issue of preference shares)			
4.	Vendor firm A/c	Dr.	1,06,000	
	To ordinary share capital A/c			1,06,000
	(Being settlement of p.c.)			

Opening balance sheet of purchasing company i.e., Ltd., Co.

Balance Sheet as on 30st Dec, 2011

Liabilities	₹	Assets	₹
Share capital:		Goodwill	40,000
10,600 ordinary		Land & buildings	50,000
Shares of Rs. 10 each	1,06,000	Machinery	12,000
9% Pref. share capital	20,000	Sy. Debtors	7,000
		Bills Receivable	5,000
		Patents	4,000
		Stock	8,000
	1,26,000		1,26,000

Illustration 9:

Amar and Bhaskar were partners sharing profits and losses equally decided to convert their business into a limited company on 31st Dec. 2011 with the following balance sheet:

Liabilities	₹	Assets		₹
Sy. creditors	20,000	Cash in hand		150
Bills payable	5,000	Bills receivable		2,500
Amar's loan A/c	10,000	Sy. debtors	30,000	
Reserve fund	3,000	Less: reserve	1,500	28,500
Capital A/cs: Amar	15,000	Stock in trade		20,000
Bhaskar	10,000	Furniture		1,850
		Machinery		6,000
		Patents		4,000
	63,000			63,000

They agreed to sell their business to Madhavacharya and Company and let them take over the assets and liabilities as follows:

Machinery Rs. 7,500, stock at ₹ 18,000, sy. debtors at ₹ 25,350; bills receivable at ₹ 2,350; furniture at ₹ 1,500 and goodwill at ₹ 3000. Patents were considered valueless and the company did not take over patents.

The Company agreed to take over sy. creditors at ₹ 19,500. Bills payable were settled at ₹ 4,200. The expenses of dissolution amounted to ₹ 150. The company issued 3,000 equity shares of ₹ 10 each as part of purchase consideration and agreed to pay the balance in cash.

You are required to prepare necessary ledger accounts to close the books of the firm.

(B.U. B.Com. Nov. 1999)

Solution 9:

Working Notes:

(1) Purchase consideration is to be based on net assets method as the information regarding assets and liabilities taken over is given.

(2) B/P is not taken over by purchasing company, rather it is settled by the firm itself at Rs. 4,200.

(3) Calculation of purchase consideration:

	₹
Agreed value of assets taken over:	
Machinery	7,500
Stock	18,000
Sy. debtors	25,350
Bills receivable	2,350
Furniture	1,500
Goodwill	3,000
Total agreed value of assets taken over	57,700
∴ Less: Total agreed value of liabilities takenover – sy. creditors	19,500
∴ Purchase consideration	38,200

(4) Mode of payment of P.C.:

	₹
(i) In 3,000 equity shares of Rs. 10 each	30,000
(ii) In cash – balancing – figure	8,200
	38,200

Ledger accounts in the books of the firm:

Dr. Realisation A/c Cr.

	₹		₹
To machinery A/c	6,000	By Res. for d. debts A/c	1,500
To furniture A/c	1,850	By sy. creditors A/c	20,000
To bills receivable A/c	2,500	By bills payable A/c	5,000
To sy. debtors A/c	30,000	By Ltd. co. A/c (purchasing co.)	38,200
To stock-in-trade A/c	20,000	By loss transferred to:	
To patents	4,000	Amar's Capital A/c 1/2	2,000
To cash A/c (BP 4200 + Exps 150)	4,350	Bhaskar's Capital A/c 1/2	2,000
	68,700		68,700

Dr. Limited Company A/c. Cr.

	₹		₹
To realisation A/c	38,200	By equity shares in Ltd., co. A/c	30,000
		By cash A/c	8,200
	38,200		38,200

Dr. Partner's capital A/c. Cr.

Particulars	Amar ₹	Bhaskar ₹	Particular	Amar ₹	Bhaskar ₹
To realisation A/c – Loss	2,000	2,000	By Balance B/d	15,000	10,000
To shares in Ltd. Co.	18,130	11,870	By Reserve Fund	1,500	1,500
			By cash/bank A/c	3,630	2,370
	20,130	13,870		20,130	13,870

Working Note No. 5

In this problem agreed ratio, i.e., ratio in which shares are to distributed among partners is not given. Hence, they should be distributed in the ratio of final claim of partners. As such, final claim each partner is ascertained as follows:

Details	Amar ₹	Bhaskar ₹
Partners capital + R.F	16,500	11,500
Less : Realisation loss	2,000	2,000
Final claim	14,500	9,500

∴ Final claim ratio = 14,500 : 9,500 or 145 : 95 or 29 : 19

Hence, shares are to be distributed among partners in 29 : 19 ratio.

$$\text{Amar} = 30{,}000 \times \frac{29}{48} = 18{,}130 \text{ (Approx)}$$

$$\text{Bhaskar} = 30{,}000 \times \frac{19}{48} = 11{,}870 \text{ (Approx)}$$

$$30{,}000$$

Dr. Cash account Cr.

	₹		₹
To balance B/d	150	By realisation A/c (B/P + Exps)	4,350
To Ltd., co. A/c	8,200	By Amar's loan	10,000
To Amar's capital A/c	3,630		
To Bhaskar capital A/c	2,370		
	14,350		14,350

Dr. Amar's loan A/c Cr.

	₹		₹
To cash A/c	10,000	By Balance B/d	10,000

Dr. Equity Shares in a Ltd. company A/c Cr.

	₹		₹
To limited company A/c	30,000	By Amar's capital A/c	18,130
		By Bhaskar's capital A/c	11,870
	30,000		30,000

Illustration 10:

A, B and C are equal partners of M/s ABC & Co. The balance sheet of the firm as at 31st Dec, 2011 was as follows:

Liabilities	₹	Assets	₹
Capital A/cs: A-	50,000	Land	50,000
B-	1,00,000	Plant & machinery	2,00,000
Loan from banks	5,00,000	Buildings	70,000
Sy. creditors	1,00,000	Stocks	3,00,000
		Sy. debtors	1,00,000
		C's capital A/c	30,000
	7,50,000		7,50,000

On that date, it was decided to convert partnership into a limited company on the following terms:

(a) Land is to be valued at Rs. 1,50,000.
(b) Plant and machinery to be valued at Rs. 2,50,000.
(c) Depreciation amounting to Rs. 20,000 to be written-off in buildings.
(d) A provision of 10% of the books value to be made for obsolete stock.
(e) A reserve for doubtful debts to be made @ 10% of details.
(f) A discount of 6% would be earned on creditors when paid out.
(g) The new company will issue 12,000 equity shares of Rs. 10 each, credited as fully paid up, such share capital being valued at 1,50,000 and the balance: to be paid by issue of 8% debentures of Rs. 100 each.

Show the necessary ledger a/cs to close the books of the ABC & Co. and also show the opening balance sheet of new Co.

(B.U. B.Com. April 2002)

Solution:

Working Notes:

(1) Among the liabilities only Sy. Cr. is taken over by purchasing co. and loan from banks is not. Hence, bank loans are to be paid by the firm itself.
(2) Calculation of purchase consideration:

	₹
Assets taken over @ agreed values:	
Land	1,50,000
Plant & Machinery	2,50,000
Building (70,000 – 20,000 sqm.)	50,000
Stock (3,00,000 – 30,000 obsolete)	2,70,000
Sy. Debtors (1,00,000 – 10,000)	90,000
Total agreed value of assets taken over	8,10,000
Less: Total agreed value of liabilities taken over:	
Sy. creditors (1,00,000 – 6% dis)	94,000
∴ Purchase consideration	7,16,000

(3) Mode of payment of purchase consideration:

	₹
(a) Issue of shares :- 12,000 equity shares of Rs. 10 each @ a premium of 2.50/- per share (i.e., 12000 × 12.50)	1,50,000
(Per share market price = $\frac{1,50,000}{12,000 \text{ shares}}$ = 12/50)	
(b) Issue of 8% debentures of Rs. 100 each for the balance (i.e., 5,660 debentures of Rs. 100 each)	5,66,000
	7,16,000

(4) Bank loan amounting to Rs. 5,00,000 is to be discharged by the firm itself as it is not taken over. Here, purchasing co. has paid purchase consideration by issue of equity shares and debentures only. Hence, it should be understood that bank loans are discharged only. Hence, it should be understood that bank loans are discharged by the issue of shares and debentures in their proportion. i.e., 1,50,000 : 5,66,000 or 150 : 566 or 75 : 283 and accordingly.

∴ Amount of shares issued towards discharge of bank loan:

$$5,00,000 \times \frac{75}{358} = 1,04,750 \text{ (Approximately)}$$

Balance in debentures i.e., 3,95,250 (Approximately) or $5,00,000 \times \frac{283}{358}$

Ledger A/cs to close the books of M/s ABC & Co.

Dr. Realisation A/c Cr.

	₹		₹
To land A/c	50,000	By sy. creditors A/c	1,00,000
To plant and machinery A/c	2,00,000	By bank loan A/c	5,00,000
To building A/c	70,000	By limited company A/c	
To stock A/c	3,00,000	(Purchasing co.)	7,16,000
To sy. debtors A/c	1,00,000		
To equity shares (bank loan)	1,04,750		
To 8% debentures (bank loan)	3,95,250		
To capital A/c (profit transfer)			
A's capital 32,000			
B's capital 32,000			
C's capital 32,000	96,000		
	13,16,000		13,16,000

Limited Company A/c.
(Purchasing company A/c

Dr.	₹		₹ Cr.
To realisation A/c	7,16,000	By Equity Shares in Ltd. co. A/c	1,5 ,000
		by 8% debentues in Ltd. c	5,6 ,000
	7,16,000		7,1 ,000

(5) Before we proceed with preparation of partner's capital A/cs we should be certain as to the ratio in which shares and debentures are to be distributed among partners. Since, the agreed ratio is not given in the problem, it is implied that they should be distributed in final claim ratio. As such final claim ratio is ascertained as under:

Particulars	A	B	C
Capitals as per B/S	+ 50,000	+ 1,00,000	– 30,000
Add: Realisation profit	32,000	32,000	+ 32,000
∴ Final claim	82,000	1,32,000	2,000

∴ Final claim ratio = 82 : 132 : 2 or 41 : 66 : 1 ratio.
Hence, distribution of shares :- (i.e., 1,50,000 – 1,04,750) = 45,250 is as under:

A = 45,250 × 41/108 = ₹ 17,180

B = 45,250 × 66/108 = ₹ 27,650

C = 45,250 × 1/108 = ₹ 420

Similarly, the debentures worth (i.e. 5,66,000 – 3,95,250) = 1,70,750 are distributed as under:

A = 41/108 × 1,70,750 = Rs. 64,820

B = 66/108 × 1,70,750 = Rs. 1,04,350 and

C = 1/108 × 1,70,750 = Rs. 1,580 respectively

Dr. Partner's capital accounts Cr.

Particulars	A	B	C	Particulars	A ₹	B ₹	C ₹
To balance B/d	–	–	30,000	By balance B/d	50,000	1,00,000	–
To equity shares in Ltd co.	17,180	27,650	420	By Realisation A/c (Profit)	32,000	32,000	32,000
To debentures in Ltd co.	64,820	1,04,350	1,580				
	82,000	1,32,000	32,000		82,000	1,32,000	32,000

Dr. Shares in Ltd. co. A/c Cr.

	₹		₹
To Limited co. A/c.	1,50,000	By Realisation A/c (Bank loans)	1,04,750
		By A's capital A/c	17,180
		By B's capital A/c	27,650
		By C's capital A/c	420
	1,50,000		1,50,000

Dr. Debentures in limited co. A/c Cr.

	₹		₹
To Limited co. A/c	5,66,000	By Realisation A/c (bank loans)	3,95,250
		By A's capital A/c	64,820
		By B's capital A/c	1,04,350
		By C's capital A/c	1,580
	5,66,000		5,66,000

In the books a A Limited company

Balance sheet as on .31-12-2011

Liabilities	₹	Assets	₹
Share capital:		Land	1,50,000
To equity shares of ₹ 10 each	1,20,000	Plant and machinery	2,50,000
Share premium	30,000	Buildings	50,000
8% debentures	5,66,000	Stock	2,70,000
Sy. creditors	94,000	Sy. debtors	90,000
	8,10,000		8,10,000

Illustration 11: Lump sum payment method and assets taken over partner) Following is the balance sheet of A, B, and C who share profits and losses in the ratio of 2:2:1

Liabilities		₹	Assets	₹
Trade creditors		1,00,000	Land and buildings	10,00,000
Reserve fund		1,00,000	Plant and machinery	5,00,000
Capitals:	A-	10,00,000	Investments	5,10,000
	B-	10,00,000	Trade debtors	6,00,000
	C-	5,00,000	Cash	90,000
		27,00,000		27,00,000

The firm was sold to a private Ltd. company for 17,50,000. The company took all assets (except debtors and investments) and assumed liabilities. 'A' is to take over 60% of debtors @ 70% and 'B' is to take over the balance of debtors @ 75%. Investments were taken over by 'B' at 2% less than its book value. Realisation expenses amounted to Rs. 10,000 borne by A & C equally. The purchase consideration was settled by issuing equity shares at face value.

Prepare ledger A/cs to close the books of the firm.

(B.U. I. Semester B.Com., Dec., 2004)

Solution 11:

Working Notes:

(1) Purchase consideration was fixed at Rs. 17,50,000.

(2) For a purchase consideration of Rs. 17,50,000, Pvt. Co. took over all assets and liabilities except debtors as under:

	₹
Land & building	10,00,000
Plant & machinery	5,00,000
Cash	90,000
Total agreed value of assets taken over	15,90,000
Less: Total agreed value of liabilities takenover – Trade credited	1,00,000
Net worth	14,90,000
Good will (Bal-figure)	2,60,000
P.C.	17,50,000

(3) Debtors not assumed by purchasing company, was taken over by A and B as under:

(a) A took over 60% debtors at 70%

$$\text{i.e. } 6{,}00{,}000 \times \frac{60}{100} = 3{,}60{,}000 \text{ @ } 70\ \% = 3{,}60{,}000 \times \frac{70}{100} = 2{,}52{,}000$$

∴ Agreed value of Dr taken over by 'A' = 2,52,000

(b) 'B' took remaining debtors of Rs. 2,40,000 (40,00,000 – 3,60,000) @ 75%,

$$\text{i.e., } 240{,}000 \times \frac{75}{100} = 1{,}80{,}000$$

∴ Agreed value of debtors taken over by B = 1,80,000.

(4) Investments not assumed by purchasing company is taken over by 'B' @ 2% less, i.e., 5,10,000 – 2% = 4,99,800

		Drs		limits
Total value of assets taken over by B	=	1,80,000	+	4,99,800
	=	Rs. 6,79,800		

(5) Realisation expenses amounting to Rs. 10,000 is agreed to be paid by 'A' and 'C' equally.

∴ Entry for this transaction is as under:

Realisation A/c	Dr.	10,000	
To A's capital			5,000
To B's capital			5,000

Ledger accounts to close the books of M/s ABC firm.

Dr. Realisation A/c Cr.

	₹		₹
To land and buildings A/c	10,00,000	By trade creditors	1,00,000
To plant and machinery A/c	5,00,000	By Pvt. Ltd co. A/c	17,50,000
To investments A/c	5,10,000	By A's capital (Debtors)	2,52,000
To trade debtors A/c	6,00,000	By B's capital A/c	6,79,800
To cash A/c	90,000	(Drs + invts)	
To A's capital A/c (expenses)	5,000		
To B's capital A/c (expenses)	5,000		
To profit transferred to:			
A's capital 2/5 – 28,720			
B's capital 2/5 – 28,720			
C's capital 1/5 – 14,360	71,800		
	27,81,800		27,81,800

(6) Since the agreed ratio, i.e., the ratio in which shares received towards purchase consideration are to distributed is not given in the problem, is implied that they have to be distributed in final claim ratio.

Dr. Partner's capital account Cr.

	A ₹	B ₹	C ₹		A ₹	B ₹	C ₹
To realisation A/c (Assets taken over)	2,52,000	6,79,800	-NIL-	By Balance B/d	10,00,000	10,00,000	5,00,000
To shares in Pvt. Ltd. Co. A/c.	8,21,720	3,88,920	5,39,360	By Realisation A/c (Profit)	28,720	28,720	14,360
				By Realisation A/c (Exps)	5,000	-	5,000
				By Reserve Fund	40,000	40,000	20,000
	10,73,720	10,68,720	5,39,360		10,73,720	10,68,720	5,39,360

Pvt. Ltd. Company A/c.
(Purchasing Company A/c)

Dr. Cr.

	₹		₹
To Realisation A/c	17,50,000	By equity shares in Pvt. Ltd., co. A/c	17,50,000
	17,50,000		17,50,000

Dr. Equity shares in Pvt. Ltd. Co. A/c Cr.

	₹		₹
To Pvt. Ltd. Co. A/c	17,50,000	By A's capital A/c	8,21,720
		By B's capital A/c	3,88,920
		By C's capital A/c	5,39,360
	17,50,000		17,50,000

Illustration 12:

The following is the summarised balance sheet of A & B, who were sharing profits and losses in the ratio of 2:1 respectively:

Liabilities	₹	Assets	₹
Capital A/cs: A	1,40,000	Fixed assets	1,40,000
B	1,00,000	Stock	70,000
B's loan	60,000	Debtors	1,30,000
Creditors	90,000	Cash at bank	50,000
	3,90,000		3,90,000

The fixed assets included 2 motor cars having book values of ₹ 16,000 and ₹ 12,000 respectively, which were taken over by A and B at agreed values of ₹ 24,000 and ₹ 16,000 respectively. They sold fixed assets (other than 2 motor cars) and stock to Sundar Ltd., at an agreed price of ₹ 3,20,000. The company agreed to pay cash of ₹ 12,000 and issue 800 preference shares of ₹ 80 each and 1,800 equity shares of ₹ 100 each at a market value of ₹ 80 each.

The debtors realised. Rs. 1,22,000 and creditors were paid Rs. 85,000 in full settlement. Preference shares were used to pay 'B' towards his loan and the balance of preference shares were given to 'A' in part payment of his amount due. Equity shares were allotted between A and B in the ratio of 5:4.

Show the necessary ledger A/cs to close the books of the firm.

(B.U. I Semester B.Com., Nov. 2005)

Solution 12

Working Notes:

(1) Two motors included in fixed assets are taken over by A & B at 24,000 and 16,000 respectively.

(2) Purchase consideration is based on remaining fixed assets and stock at Rs. 3,20,000.

(3) Mode of payment of purchase consideration:

		₹
(a)	Cash Payment	1,12,000
(b)	Issue of 800 preference shares of Rs. 80 each	64,000
(c)	Issue of 1,800 equity shares of Rs. 100 each @ market value of Rs. 80/- per share (1,800 × 80)	1,44,000
		3,20,000

(4) Debtors not assumed by Sundar Ltd., realised for Rs. 1,22,000 similarly, creditors not assumed by Sundar Ltd., were settled at Rs. 85,000 in full settlement.

Ledger A/cs to close the books of M/s AB Firm

Dr. Realisation A/c Cr.

	₹		₹
To fixed assets A/c	1,40,000	By creditors A/c	90,000
To stock A/c	70,000	By sundar Ltd A/c	3,20,000
To debtors A/c	1,30,000	By A's capital (M-Car)	24,000
To bank A/c – (crs paid)	85,000	By B's capital (M-Car)	16,000
To profit transferred to:		By bank A/c (Drs)	1,22,000
A's capital A/c 2/3 98,000			
B's capital A/c 1/3 49,000	1,47,000		
	5,72,000		5,72,000

Dr. Sundar Ltd. A/c (Purchasing Co.) Cr.

	₹		₹
To realisation A/c	3,20,000	By bank A/c	1,12,000
		By pref. shares in Sundar Ltd. A/c	64,000
		By equity shares in Sundar Ltd.	1,44,000
	3,20,000		3,20,000

(5) Preference shares were to be issued towards discharge of B's loan and balance towards part settlement of A's dues.

Dr. B's loan A/c Cr.

	₹		₹
To pref. shares in Sundar Ltd.	60,000	By Balance B/d	60,000
	60,000		60,000

Dr. Partner's capital A/c Cr.

Particulars	A ₹	B ₹	Particulars	A ₹	B ₹
To Realisation A/c – (M-cars)	24,000	16,000	By Balance B/d	1,40,000	1,00,000
To preference shares in Sundar Ltd., (64,000 – 60,000)	4,000	-	By Realisation A/c – Profit	98,000	49,000
To Equity shares in Sundar Ltd. in 5:4 ratio	80,000	64,000			
To Bank A/c Balance	1,30,000	69,000			
	2,38,000	1,49,000		2,38,000	1,49,000

Dr. Bank A/c Cr.

	₹		₹
To Balance B/d	50,000	By Realisation A/c (creditors)	85,000
To Sunder Ltd. A/c	1,12,000	By A's capital A/c	1,30,000
To Realisation A/c (Debtors)	1,22,000	By B's capital A/c	69,000
	2,84,000		2,84,000

Illustration 13

Alpha and Beta were in partnership sharing profits and losses in the ratio of 3:1. The following is the balance sheet of the firm as at 31st March, 2011.

Liabilities	₹	Assets	₹
Capital A/cs : Alpha	28,200	Fixed assets	21,000
Beta	10,000	Stock	11,200
Beta's loan	3,000	Sundry debtors	19,600
Sy. creditors	14,320	Cash at bank	3,720
	55,520		55,520

Mega Ltd., agrced to take over stock and fixed assets excluding the value of motor car ₹ 4,100 (included fixed assets) for a consideration of ₹ 48,000 which is to be satisfied by the payment of cash ₹ 16,000, allotment of 160 preference share of ₹ 100 each valued at ₹ 75 per share and the balance by the allotment of ₹ 1,600 equity shares of the face value of ₹ 10 each at ₹ 12/50 per share.

The debts realised ₹ 19,200 and creditors were settled for ₹ 14,000.

The following were agreed between partners:

(a) The equity shares should be allotted in their profit sharing ratio.

(b) Alpha to take over the motor car at an agreed value of Rs. 4200.

(c) The preference shares to be allotted to Beta to the value of his loan and the balance to be allotted equally between the partners.

(d) The balance remaining to be settled in cash.

Prepare Realisation A/c, Partner's capital A/c and Bank A/c in the books of Alpha and Beta.

(B.U. I Semester, B.Com. Nov. 2009)

Solution:

Working Notes:

(1) Mega Ltd. took over fixed assets excluding motor car & stock for Rs. 48,000. ∴ Purchase consideration = ₹ 48,000.

(2) Mega Ltd. agreed to pay purchase consideration as under:

		₹
(a)	Cash payment	16,000
(b)	Issue of 160 pref. shares of Rs. 100 each @ 75/- per share – (160 × 75)	12,000
(c)	Issue of 1600 equity shares of Rs. 10 each at Rs. 12/50 per share	20,000
		48,000

In the books of Alpha and Beta – Ledger A/cs

Dr. Realisation A/c Cr.

	₹		₹
To fixed assets A/c	21,000	By creditors A/c	14,320
To stock A/c	11,200	by Mega Co. A/c	48,000
To debtors A/c	19,600	By Alpha's capital A/c (motor car)	4,200
To bank A/c – crs	14,000	By bank A/c – Drs.	19,200
To profit transferred to: Alpha's capital ¾ 14,940; Beta's capital ¼ 4,980	19,920		
	85,720		85,720

Dr. Mega Ltd. A/cs. Cr.

	₹		₹
To realisation A/c	48,000	By bank A/c	16,000
		By pre shares in Mega Co. A/c	12,000
		By equity shares in Mega Co. A/c	20,000
	48,000		48,000

Dr. Partner's capital A/c Cr.

Particulars	Alpha	Beta	Particular	Alpha ₹	Beta ₹
To realisation A/c – (M-car)	4,200	-	By balance B/d	28,200	10,000
To preference shares in Mega Co. (12,000 – 3,000) in 1:1 ratio	4,500	4,500	By realisation A/c profit	14,940	4,980
To Equity shares in Mega Co. (3:1)	15,000	5,000			
To Bank A/c	19,440	5,480			
	43,140	14,980		43,140	14,980

Dr. Beta's loan A/c Cr.

	₹		₹
To pref. shares in Mega Ltd.	3,000	By Balance B/d	3,000
	3,000		3,000

Cash at Bank A/c

Dr. Cr.

	₹		₹
To balance B/d	3,720	By realisation A/c (Crs)	14,000
To realisation A/c – Drs.	19,200	By Alpha's Capital	19,440
To Mega Co. A/c	16,000	By Beta's Capital	5,480
	38,920		38,920

Illustration 14:

Venkat and Suresh are equal partners and desire to convert their partnership into a limited company. This balance sheet as 31st Dec, 2011 was as under:

Balance sheet

Liabilities	₹	Assets	₹
Sy. creditors	37,000	Stock	20,000
Loans	25,000	Sy. debtors	47,000
General reserve	15,000	Machinery	15,000
Capitals : Venkat	20,000	Buildings	35,000
Suresh	20,000		
	1,17,000		1,17,000

The following terms were agreed upon:

(a) The loan creditors have agreed to take preference shares in the new company.

(b) The creditors were to be paid in cash.

(c) Machinery and buildings were to be taken at the agreed values of ₹ 20,000 and ₹ 55,000 respectively.

(d) 9% debentures were to be issued for cash to the extent of ₹ 1,00,000.

(e) The goodwill of the firm is to be valued at ₹ 20,000

(f) The company to allot equity shares to the vendor for the purchase consideration.

You are requested to give the Realisation Account, Partner's capital accounts to close the books of the firm and opening Balance Sheet of a new company after passing incorporation entries.

(B.U. I. B.Com. Nov. 1999)

Solution 14

Working Notes:

(1) In this problem, the agreed ratio for distribution of equity shares received from purchasing company is not given. Hence, it is implied that they should be distributed in Final Claim Ratio. Since, Profit sharing ratio and capitals of the partners are equal, the final claim ratio also be equal. As such, equity shares are to be distributed equally between the partners.

(2) It is stated in the problem that loan creditors and creditors are satisfied by purchasing company by issue of shares and payment of cash respectively. Therefore, both loan creditors & credited should be deducted from Agreed value of assets takenover.

(3) Calculation of Purchase Consideration

	₹
Agreed value of Assets taken over:	
Goodwill	20,000
Machinery	20,000
Buildings	55,000
Sy. Debtors	47,000
Stock	20,000
∴ Total Agreed value of Assets taken over:	1,62,000
Less: Total agreed value of liabilities taken over:	
Loan crs. – 25,000	
Sy. creditors 37,000	62,000
∴ Purchase consideration	1,00,000

(4) Regarding taking over over of stock and debtors it is not clear in the problem. Hence, it is assumed that they have been taken over book values.

Ledger Accounts to close the books of Venkat & Suresh Firm

Dr. Realisation A/c Cr.

	₹		₹
To stock A/c	20,000	By sy. creditors A/c	37,000
To sy. debtors A/c	47,000	By loan creditors A/c	25,000
To machinery A/c	15,000	By limited company A/c	1,00,000
To buildings A/c	35,000		
To profit transferred to :-			
Venkat capital 22,500			
Suresh's capital 22,500	45,000		
	1,62,000		1,62,000

Dr. Limited Company A/c (Purchasing company) Cr.

	₹		₹
To realisation A/c	1,00,000	By equity share in Ltd. company A/c	1,00,000
	1,00,000		1,00,000

Dr. Partner's capital account Cr.

Particulars A/c	Venkat ₹	Suresh ₹	Particular	Venkat ₹	Suresh ₹
To equity shares in Ltd. company A/c	50,000	50,000	By balance B/d	20,000	20,000
			By realisation A/c – profit	22,500	22,500
			By general reserve	7,500	7,500
	50,000	50,000		50,000	50,000

Incorporation journal entries in the books of purchasing company

	Particulars	L.F.	Dr. ₹	Cr. ₹
1.	Business purchase A/c Dr.		1,00,000	
	To vendor firm A/c			1,00,000
	(Being purchase of business of a firm)			

(Contd.)

(Contd.)

2.	Goodwill A/c Dr. Machinery A/c Dr. Buildings A/c Dr. Sy. Debtors A/c Dr. Stock A/c Dr. To loans A/c To sy. Creditors A/c To business purchase A/c (Being incorporation of assets and liabilities taken over from the firm)		20,000 20,000 55,000 47,000 20,000	 25,000 37,000 1,00,000
3.	Cash A/c Dr. To 9% Debentures A/c (being the fresh issue of 9% Debentures)		1,00,000	 1,00,000
4.	Loans A/c Dr. To preference shares capital A/c Dr. (Being discharge of loan by the issue of shares)		25,000	 25,000
5.	Sy. Creditors A/c Dr. To cash A/c (Being discharge of amount due to creditors)		37,000	 37,000
6.	Vendor firm A/c Dr. To equity share capital A/c (Being purchase consideration paid by the issue of equity shares)		1,00,000	 1,00,000

Balance Sheet of Ltd. Co.
As on 1st January, 2012

Liabilities	₹	Assets	₹
Share capital:		Goodwill	20,000
Equity share capital	1,00,000	Machinery	20,000
Preference share capital	25,000	Buildings	55,000
9% Debentures	1,00,000	Sy. debtors	47,000
		Stocks	20,000
		Cash balance (1,00,000 – 37,000)	63,000
	2,25,000		2,25,000

Illustration 15: Lump Sum Payment Method and Treatment of Partner's Current Accounts

A, B and C share profits and losses of business as to 1/2, 1/3 and 1/6 respectively. Their balance sheet as on 31st Dec, 2011 was as follows:

Liabilities		₹	Assets		₹
Capital A/cs:	A	70,000	Goodwill		10,000
	B	80,000	Land		20,000
	C	10,000	Buildings		1,10,000
General reserve		18,000	Machinery		50,000
Investment fluctuating Fund		4,000	Motor car		28,000
C's loan A/c		33,000	Furniture		12,000
Mrs. A's Loan A/c		15,000	Investments		18,000
Trade creditors		76,000	Loose tools		7,000
Creditors for expenses		20,000	Stocks		18,000
Bills payable		14,000	Bills receivable		20,000
Bank overdraft		60,000	Sy. debtors	40,000	
			Less: Provision	2,000	38,000
			Cash at bank		1,000
			C's current A/c		56,000
			Profit and loss A/c		12,000
		4,00,000			4,00,000

The partners decide to convert their firm into joint stock company. For this purpose ABC Ltd., was formed with an authorized capital of ₹ 10,00,000 divided into ₹ 100 equity shares. The business of the firm was sold to this company as at the date of balance sheet given above on the following terms:

(i) Motor car, furniture, investments, loose tools, debtors and cash are not to be taken over by the company.

(ii) Liabilities for bills payable and bank overdraft are to be taken over by the company.

(iii) The purchase price is settled at ₹ 1,95,500 payable as to ₹ 75,500 in cash, and the balance in company's fully paid shares of ₹ 100 each.

The remaining assets and liabilities of the firm are directly disposed of by the firm as per the details given below:

Investments are taken over by 'A' for ₹ 13,000; debtors realise in all ₹ 20,000; motor car, furniture and loose tools fetch ₹ 24,000, ₹ 4,000 and ₹ 1000 respectively. 'A' agrees to pay his wife's loan and the creditors were paid ₹ 74,000 in full settlement of their claims. Creditors for expenses were paid-off in full. The realisation expenses amounted to ₹ 500.

The equity shares received from the company are to be divided among partners in profit sharing ratio.

You are required to show necessary ledger accounts.

(Delhi University B.Com (Hons) adopted)

Solution:

Working Notes

(1) Purchase consideration is given in the problem itself as Rs. 1,95,500.

(2) Mode of payment of purchase consideration:

	₹
(a) Cash payment (as given)	75,500
(b) Issue of equity shares (Bal-fig.) i.e., 1,200 equity shares of Rs. 100 each fully paid	1,20,000
	1,95,500

(3) Equity shares received firm purchasing co. (ABC Co.) to be distributed in profit sharing ratio (agreed ratio) as given in the problem itself.

Ledger accounts in the books M/s ABC partnership firm:

Dr. Realisation A/c Cr.

		₹			₹
To goodwill A/c		10,000	By provision for bad debts		2,000
To land A/c		20,000	By trade creditors A/c		76,000
To building A/c		1,10,000	By creditors for expenses A/c		20,000
To machinery A/c		50,000	By bills payable A/c		14,000
To motor car A/c		28,000	By bank overdraft A/c		60,000
To furniture A/c		12,000	By Mrs. A's loan A/c		15,000
To investment A/c		18,000	By ABC Co. Ltd A/c		1,95,500
To loose Tools A/c		7,000	By A's capital A/c (invests)		13,000
To stock A/c		18,000	By Bank A/c (sale of assets not taken over)		
To bills Receivable A/c		20,000	Debtors	20,000	
To sy. debtors A/c		40,000	M-Car	24,000	
To A's capital – (Mrs A's Loan) A/c		15,000	Furniture	4,000	
			Loose tools	1,000	49,000
To Bank A/c :					
Crs (trade)	74,000				
Crs for exps	20,000				
Realisation exps	500	94,500			
To profit transferred to:					
A's Capital	1,000				
B's Capital	667				
C's Capital	333	2,000			
		4,44,500			4,44,500

Purchasing Company A/c
ABC Company Limited A/c

Dr. Cr.

	₹		₹
To realistation A/c	1,95,500	By Cash A/c	75,500
		By Equity Shares in ABC Ltd. A/c	1,20,000
	1,95,500		1,95,500

Dr. Partner's Capital Accounts Cr.

Particulars	A ₹	B ₹	C ₹	Particulars	A ₹	B ₹	C ₹
To C's current A/c	-	-	56,000	By Balance B/d	70,000	80,000	10,000
To Profit and Loss A/c (Loss)	6,000	4,000	2,000	By General Reserve	9,000	6,000	3,000
To Realisation A/c – invst	13,000	-	-	By I.F. Fund A/c	2,000	1,333	667
To Equity shares in ABC Ltd. (3:2:1)	60,000	40,000	20,000	By Realisation A/c (Mrs. A's Loan)	15,000	-	-
To Bank A/c	18,000	44,000	-	By Realisation A/c (Profit)	1,000	667	333
				By Bank A/c			64,000
	97,000	88,000	78,000		97,000	88,000	78,000

Dr. C's Loan A/c Cr.

	₹		₹
To Bank A/c	33,000	By Balance B/d	33,000
	33,000		33,000

Dr. Bank A/c Cr.

	₹		₹
To balance B/d	1,000	By Realisation A/c (traders + crs for exps + Realisation exps)	94,500
To ABC Co. Ltd. A/c (PC)	75,500	By C's loan A/c	33,000
To realisation A/c (assets realised)	49,000	By A's capital A/c	18,000
To C's capital A/c	64,000	By B's capital	44,000
	1,89,500		1,89,500

Illustration 16: (When Capitals are fixed)

Ram and Shyam in partnership sharing profits and losses in the ratio of 3:1. The following is the balance sheet of the firm as on 31st Dec. 2011.

Liabilities	₹	Assets	₹
Capital A/cs:-		Fixed assets	31,500
Ram	36,000	Stocks	16,800
Shyam	12,000	Debtors	29,400
Current A/cs:-		Bank	5,580
Ram	6,300		
Shyam	3,000		
Loan from Shyam	4,500		
Sy. Crs.	21,480		
	83,280		83,280

The Prakash Ltd. agreed to take over stock and fixed assets exchanging the value of motor car ₹ 6,150 for a consideration of ₹ 72,000 which is to be satisfied:

(a) by the payment of cash ₹ 24,000.

(b) by allotment of 240 preference shares of ₹ 100 each valued at ₹ 75 per share and

(c) the balance by the allotment of ₹ 2,400 equity shares of the face value of ₹ 10 each.

The debtors realised ₹ 28,800 and the creditors were settled for ₹ 21,000

It was agreed between the partners as follows:-

(a) Equity shares be allotted in their fixed capital ratio.

(b) Ram to take over motor car at an agreed value of ₹ 6,300.

(c) The preference shares be allotted to Shyam to the value of loan amount and remaining preference shares be allotted to partner's equally.

(d) The balance remaining be paid in cash.

Prepare necessary ledger A/cs to close the books of the firm and also a statement showing distribution of shares between Partners.

(B.Com. K.U. Dharwad adopted)

Solution

Working Notes:

1) Purchase consideration is fixed at ₹ 72,000 for taking over stock and fixed assets other than a motor car worth ₹ 6,150 included in fixed assets.

2) Mode of Payment of Purchase Consideration

(a) Cash Payment ———	24,000
(b) Issue of Shares :-	
(i) 240 preference shares of ₹ 100 each, @ ₹ 75 per share (i.e., 240 × 75)	18,000
(ii) 2,400 equity shares of ₹ 10 each for the balance (i.e., 30,000 ÷ 2,400 share) at ₹ 12/50 per share	30,000
	72,000

Ledger accounts to close the books of Ram and Shyam Firm:

Dr. Realisation A/c Cr.

	₹		₹
To fixed assets A/c	31,500	By sy. creditors A/c	21,480
To stock A/c	16,800	By Prakash Ltd. A/c	72,000
To sy. debtors A/c	29,400	By bank A/c (drs realised)	28,800
To bank A/c: (crs)	21,000	By Ram's capital A/c (motor car)	6,300
To profit transferred to :			
Ram's capital ¾ - 22,410			
Shyam's capital ¼ - 7,470	29,880		
	1,28,580		1,28,580

Dr. Prakash Ltd. A/c of (Purchasing Company A/c) Cr.

	₹		₹
To realisation A/c	72,000	By bank A/c	24,000
		By preference shares in Prakash Ltd., A/c	18,000
		By equity shares in Prakash Ltd. A/c	30,000
	72,000		72,000

Dr. Partner's Capital Account Cr.

Particulars	Ram	Shyam	Particulars	Ram	Shyam
To realisation A/c (Motor Car)	6,300	-	By balance B/d	36,000	12,000
To preference shares in Prakash Ltd. (18000-4,500) equally	6,750	6,750	By current A/cs – (Transfer)	6,300	3,000
			By realisation A/c (profit)	22,410	7,470
To equity shares in Prakash Ltd. (3:1)	22,500	7,500			
To bank A/c	29,160	8,220			
	64,710	22,470		64,710	22,470

(3) Equity shares are distributed in fixed Capital ratio i.e., 36,000 : 12,000 or 3:1

Dr. Bank A/c Cr.

	₹		₹
To balance B/d – To realisation A/c – (Drs) To Prakash Ltd. A/c	5,580 28,800 24,000	By realisation A/c – (crs) By Ram's capital A/c By Shyam's capital A/c	21,000 29,160 8,220
	58,380		58,380

Dr. Shyam's loan A/c Cr.

	₹		₹
To preference shares in Prakash Ltd.	4,500	By balance B/d	4,500
	4,500		4,500

Statement showing distribution of shares between partners

	Particulars	Ram ₹	Shyam ₹
1.	Distribution of preference shares: Out of 240 shares received from Prakash Ltd., 4500 worth shares were issued towards Shyam's loan i.e., 60 shares (4500/75) and the balance of 180 shares worth Rs. 13,500 distributed equally i.e., 90 shares each to both partners	6,750	6,750
2.	Distribution of equity shares in fixed capital ratio i.e., 36,000 : 12,000 or 3:1 = Out of 2400 shares Ram will get 1800 shares & Shyam 600 shares @ Rs. 12/50 per share	22,500	7,500
		29,250	14,250

Illustration 17: *(Fixed capital's – Lump Sum Payment)*

Ravi and Gavi were in partnership sharing profits and losses in the ratio of 2/3 and 1/3. The summarized balance sheet of the firm as on 31st December, 2011 was as follows:

Liabilities	₹	Assets	₹
Capital A/cs : Ravi :	50,000	Fixed Assets	70,000
Gavi :	40,000	Current Assets:-	
Current A/cs:		Stocks	35,000
Ravi 20,000		Book Debts	65,000
Less: Gavi 10,000	10,000	Bank Balance	15,000
Gavi's loan A/c	30,000		
Sundry creditors	55,000		
	1,85,000		1,85,000

The fixed assets included 2 motor cars, having book value of Rs. 8,000 and Rs. 6,000 respectively.

The partners desiring to retire from the business, accepted the offer of National Company Ltd., to acquire stock and fixed assets, other than motor cars at an agreed purchase price of Rs. 1,60,000.

The purchase consideration was to be satisfied by a cash payment of Rs. 56,000, the allotment by the company to the partners of 400, 5% preference shares of Rs. 100 each and the balance by the allotment by the company to the partners of 900 equity shares of Rs. 100 each.

The debtors realised Rs. 61,000 and creditors settled for Rs. 51,000.

The partners agreed that the following should be the basis of distribution on dissolution of partnership:

(1) Ravi to take over one car at a valuation of Rs. 12,000 and Gavi the other at Rs. 8,000.

(2) Ravi to be allotted preference shares of the value of Rs. 2,000, the reminder to be allotted to Gavi.

(3) The equity shares to be allotted in the proportion of fixed capitals.

(4) Both the preference and equity shares to be valued at Rs. 80 per share.

(5) The balance to be settled in cash.

You are required to prepare: (a) Realisation A/c (b) Bank A/c and Partner's capital accounts, showing the final settlement between partners.

(C.A. (Inter) adopted)

Solution:

Working Notes:

(1) The purchase price is fixed at Rs. 1,60,000 for taking over stock and fixed assets other than motor cars included therein fixed assets.

	₹
(2) Mode of payment of purchase price:	
(a) Cash payment	56,000
(b) Issue of shares:	
(i) 400, 5% preference shares of Rs. 100 each @ Rs. 80 per share	32,000

(ii) 900 equity shares of Rs. 100 each @ Rs. 80 per share	72,000
Total Purchased Price	1,60,000

(3) In the absence of agreed ratio given in the problem for distribution of shares, shares and debentures would have been distributed in fixed capital ratio.

As agreed ratio is given, shares & debentures are to be distributed accordingly.

Ledger accounts to close the books of Ravi and Gavi firm

Dr. Reallisation A/c Cr.

	₹		₹
To fixed assets A/c	70,000	By sy. creditors	55,000
To stock A/c	35,000	By national company A/c	1,60,000
To book-debts A/c	65,000	By Ravi's capital A/c (motor car)	12,000
To bank A/c – (sy. creditors)	51,000	By Gavi's captial A/c (motor car)	8,000
To profit transferred to:		By bank A/c (drs realised)	61,000
Ravi's capital 2/3 × 75,000	50,000		
Gavi's capital 1/3 × 75,000	25,000		
	2,96,000		2,96,000

Dr. Partner's capital account Cr.

Particulars	Ravi	Gavi	Particulars	Ravi	Gavi
To Current A/c (Transfer)	–	10,000	By Balance B/d	50,000	40,000
To Realisation A/c (M-car)	12,000	8,000	By Current A/c (Transfer)	20,000	–
To 5% Preference Shares in National Co. Ltd.,	2,000	–	By Realisation A/c (Profit)	50,000	25,000
To Equity shares in National Co. Ltd. A/c (5:4)	40,000	32,000			
To Bank A/c – Balance	66,000	15,000			
	1,20,000	65,000		1,20,000	65,000

Dr. National company Ltd. A/c Cr.

	₹		₹
To realisation A/c	1,60,000	By Bank A/c	56,000
		By 5% pref. shares in national Co. Ltd. A/c	32,000
		By equity shares in national co. ltd. A/c	72,000
	1,60,000		1,60,000

Gavi Loan A/c

Dr. Cr.

	₹		₹
To 5% pref. shares in national co. Ltd. A/c	30,000	By balance B/d	30,000
	30,000		30,000

Bank account

Dr. Cr.

	₹		₹
To balance B/d	15,000	By realisation A/c – (crs)	51,000
To national co. Ltd. A/c	56,000	By Ravi's capital	66,000
To realisation A/c – Drs	61,000	By Gavi's capital	15,000
	1,32,000		1,32,000

Illustration 18: *(Lump sum payment and fixed capitals)*
Rama, Lakshmana and Bharatha were in partnership sharing profits and losses in the ratio of 3:2:1.

The Partnership balance sheet as on 31st December, 2011 was as follows:

Liabilities	₹	Assets	₹
Capital A/cs: Rama	75,000	Fixed assets:	
Laxmana	45,000	Plant and machinery	1,20,000
Bharatha	30,000	Motor car	30,000
Current A/cs:		Current assets:-	
Rama	7,500	Stocks	42,000
Laxmana	22,500	Debtors	90,000
Shathrugna's loan A/c	15,000	Cash in hand	2,250
Creditors	66,000	Current A/c – Bharatha	6,750
Bank overdraft	30,000		
	2,91,000		2,91,000

All the partners wish to retire from the firm had agreed to accept an offer from Nav Bharath Company Limited, to acquire assets of their business for Rs. 1,95,000 with the exception of debtors and cash balance and motor car.

The consideration was to be satisfied as follows:

(1) 450 10% preference shares of Rs. 100 each at par
(2) 1,350 equity shares of Rs. 50 each valued at Rs. 100 each and the balance in cash.

The debtors realised Rs. 63,000 and creditors were settled at Rs. 58,500.

The partners agreed that basis of distribution on the winding up partnership firm was to be as follows :

(1) Lakshmana to take over motor car retained by the firm at on agreed value of Rs. 21,000.
(2) Shatrugna's loan to be taken over by Lakshmana.
(3) The equity shares to be allotted in the ratio of fixed capitals.
(4) The preference shares to be allotted in their profit sharing ratio.
(5) The balance (if any) due to the partners to be settled in cash.

You are required to prepare necessary ledger A/cs to close the books of the firm.

Solution

Working Notes:

(1) Purchase consideration is fixed at Rs. 1,95,000 for taking over stock and plant and machinery only.
(2) Mode of payment of purchase consideration:

(i) Issue of:	
(a) 450, 10% preference shares of Rs. 100 each.	45,000
(b) 1,350 equity shares of Rs. 50 each @ premium of Rs. 50 per share (1350 × 100)	1,35,000
(ii) Balance – in cash	15,000
∴ Purchase Price	1,95,000

Ledger accounts to close the books of the firm:

Dr. Realisation A/c Cr.

		₹		₹
To plant machinery A/c		1,20,000	By sy. creditors A/c	66,000
To motor car A/c		30,000	By bank overdraft A/c	30,000
To stock A/c		42,000	By Nav Bharath Co. Ltd. A/c	1,95,000
To sy. debtors		90,000	By cash A/c – (debtors)	63,000
To cash A/c:			By Laxman's capital A/c (motor car)	21,000
CRS	58,500			
BOD	30,000	88,500		
To profit transferred to:				
Rama's A/c 3/6	2,250			
Laxmana's A/c 2/6	1,500			
Bharatha's A/c 1/6	750	4,500		
		3,75,000		3,75,000

Dr. Nav Bharath Co. Ltd. A/c Cr.

	₹		₹
To Realisation A/c	1,95,000	By preference shares in Nav Bharath Co. A/c	45,000
		By equity shares in Nav Bharath Co.	1,35,000
		By cash A/c	15,000
	1,95,000		1,95,000

Dr. Partner's capital A/cs Cr.

Particulars	Rama ₹	Laxmana ₹	Bharatha ₹	Particulars	Rama ₹	Laxmana ₹	Bharatha ₹
To current A/c – (transfer)	-	-	6,750	By balance B/d	75,000	45,000	30,000
To realisation A/c motor car	-	21,000	-	By current A/cs (transfer)	7,500	22,500	-
To equity shares in new Bharath Co. A/c (5:3:2)	67,500	40,500	27,000	By Realisation A/c (Profit)	2,250	1,500	750
To preference shares (in 3:2:1)	22,500	15,000	7,500	By shatrugan's loan	-	15,000	-
To cash A/c	-	7,500	-	By cash A/c	5,250	-	10,500
	90,000	84,000	41,250		90,000	84,000	41,250

Dr. Cash A/c Cr.

	₹		₹
To balance B/d	2,250	By realisation A/c (CRS + BOD)	88,500
To Nav Bharath Co. Ltd. A/c	15,000	By Laxman's capital A/c	7,500
To realisation A/c (Debtors)	63,000		
To Rama's capital A/c	5,250		
To Bharath's capital A/c	10,500		
	96,000		96,000

EXERCISES

Section – A

(1) What is realisation A/c?

(2) When do you prepare realisation A/c?

(3) What is the nature of realisation A/c?

(4) How do you prepare realisation A/c?
(5) How do you close realisation A/c?
(6) State any 2 differences between realisation A/c and revaluation A/c?
(7) What is purchase consideration?
(8) Mention 2 methods of calculating purchase consideration?
(9) Give any two reasons for conversion a firm into a company?
(10) State in which ratio should the debentures received in purchase price be distributed among partners?
(11) What is goodwill in the context of sale of a firm to a company?
(12) State two objectives of a sale of a firm to a company?
(13) How do you close realisation A/c having credit balance?
(14) Write an entry to close realisation showing debit balance?
(15) How do you distribute the shares and debentures received from P. company as purchase consideration among the partners?
(16) What is final claim ratio?
(17) What is agreed ratio?
(18) How do you treat the assets and liabilities not taken over by purchasing company?
(19) What entry you pass for realisation expenses agreed to be paid by a partner?
(20) Distinguish between a share and debenture?
(21) How do you ascertain purchase consideration under net asset method?
(22) What are the different methods of discharging the purchase consideration due by purchasing company?
(23) What is the effect of conversion of partnership into a company?
(24) What journal entry you pass in the books of purchasing company for purchase of assets and liabilities of a firm?
(25) What do you mean by incorporation journal entries?
(26) Bring out two advantages in converting a partnership into a limited company?
(27) The purchase company does not take over the following:
 (a) Investments which are realizable
 (b) Goodwill considered worthless.
 How will a vendor company treat them in the books of accounts.

Section – B

(1) Distinguish between realisation account and revaluate account?
(2) Pass incorporation journal entries in the books of the company from the following details:
 Purchase consideration = ₹ 11,25,000 value of sundry assets taken over Rs. 13,50,000, current liabilities taken over = ₹ 1,35,000, settlement of purchase consideration = 60 % in equity shares of ₹ 10 each at face value and the balance in 8% debentures of Rs. 100 each at par.
 (B.U. I. Sem. B.Com. Dec, 2007)

(3) Calculate the amount of purchase consideration from the following: Purchase company agreed to issue 60,000 equity shares o Rs. 10 each valued at Rs. 12 cash. 24,000, 8% debentures of Rs. 10 each at a discount of 5%, pay cash equal to 10% of face value of shares and debentures issued.

The company also agreed to meet the dissolution expenses of Rs. 10,000

(B.U. I. Sem. B.Com. Dec, 2007)

(4) Calculate the amount of purchase consideration from the following details:

The purchasing company agreed to issue 20,000 equity shares of ₹ 10 each at 12/50 per share, 1000 9% preference shares of ₹ 100 each at par, 1000 6% debentures of ₹ 100 each at a discount of 10% and pay equal to 20% of the total purchase consideration.

(B.U. I.Sem. B.Com. Dec, 2008)

(5) What is the accounting procedure involved in conversion of partnership firm into a company?

(6) What are the merits of converting partnership firm into a limited company?

Section – C

(1) A and B are partners having profit sharing ratio of 2:1 and their balance sheet as on 31st Dec, 2011 was as follows:

Liabilities	Amount	Assets		Amount
Creditors	1,20,000	Cash		900
B/P	30,000	Sy. debtors	1,80,000	
Reserve fund	18,000	Less: reserve	9,000	1,71,000
A/c's loan	60,000	B/R		15,000
Capitals: A	90,000	Stock		1,31,100
B	60,000	Machinery		60,000
	3,78,000			3,78,000

They agreed to sell their business to a limited company and the company to take over the assets and liabilities as follows:

Machinery at ₹ 48,000, stock at ₹ 1,05,000, debtors at ₹ 1,52,100, B/R at ₹ 15,000, and goodwill at ₹ 18,000. The company agreed to take over creditors at ₹ 1,14,000 and B/P at ₹ 30,000. The firm received ₹ 1,20,000 of the purchase consideration in ₹ 10 fully paid equity shares and the balance in cash. Distribute the shares as per original capital ratio.

Prepare necessary ledger A/cs to close the books of the firm.

(B.U. I. Sem. B.Com. Dec. 2007)

(2) X and Y were in partnership sharing profits and losses in the ratio of 3:2. The following was the balance sheet of the firm as on 31st March, 2011.

Liabilities	Amount	Assets	Amount
Sundry creditors	26,000	Cash	12,000
X's loan	4,000	Sundry debtors	30,000
Capitals: X	60,000	Stock	38,000
Y	30,000	Fixed assets	40,000
	1,20,000		1,20,000

'Z' Co. Ltd, agreed to take over the fixed assets and stock a consideration of Rs. 80,000 which is to be satisfied:

(a) by payment of cash Rs. 16,000.

(b) by allotment of 240 8% preference shares of Rs. 100 each.

(c) by allotment of 32,00 equity shares of Rs. 10 each valued at Rs. 12/50 per share.

The debtors realised Rs. 28,000 and the creditors were paid Rs. 24,000 in full settlement. It was agreed between the partners as follows:

(i) Equity shares are to be allotted in their profit sharing ratio

(ii) Preference shares to be allotted to X to the value of his loan A/c and remaining preference shares to be allotted to partners equally.

Prepare necessary ledger A/cs in the books of X and Y firm

(B.U. I. Sem. B.Com. Dec. 2008)

(3) Ajay and Vijay sharing profits and losses equally decided to convert their business into a Ltd. Co.

Balance sheet as on 31.12.2011

Liabilities	Amount	Assets	Amount
Sundry creditors	24,000	Bank	33,000
Mrs. Ajay's loan	20,000	Book – debts	12,000
Bank overdraft	8,000	Stock	8,000
Reserve fund	3,000	Trade marks	4,000
Capitals: Ajay	20,000	Plant	8,000
Vijay	20,000	Buildings	30,000
	95,000		95,000

The company has agreed to take over assets as follows:

Buildings Rs. 52,000, plant at Rs. 6,000. Goodwill at Rs. 36,000. Company will not take over Mrs. Ajay's loan and bank overdraft, other assets (except) bank are taken over at book value. Vendors allotted equity shares of Rs. 10 each to the amount equivalent to purchase consideration.

Prepare realisation A/c, capital accounts of partners and bank A/c. Show calculation of purchase consideration.

(B.U. B.Com. April 2011)

(4) Arun and Kiran sharing profits and losses equally decided to convert their business into a Ltd., company on 31st Dec. 2011 on which date their balance sheet stood as follows:

Liabilities	Amount	Assets	Amount
Sundry creditors	48,000	Cash	66,000
Loan creditors	40,000	Sundry debtors	14,000
Bank overdraft	16,000	B/R	10,000
Reserve fund	6,000	Stock	16,000
Capitals A/cs: Arun	40,000	Patents	8,000
Kiran	40,000	Machinery	16,000
		Land and buildings	60,000
	1,90,000		1,90,000

The company agreed to take over the assets and liabilities at the valuating shown below:

(1) Goodwill of the firm will be valued at 2 years purchase of the average profits of the previous 3 years. Profits of the last 3 years are as follows: 2008 – ₹ 30,000; 2009 – ₹ 36,000 and ₹ 2010 – ₹ 42,000.

(2) The company will take over loan creditors by offering 8% preference shares.

(3) The company will not take over sy. creditors and bank overdraft.

(4) Land and building valued a Rs. 1,04,000 machinery at Rs. 12,000 and all other assets (except) cash at book value.

(5) Vendors were allotted ordinary shares of Rs. 10 each to the amount equivalent purchase consideration.

Prepare necessary ledger A/cs to close the books of the firm.

(B.U. B.Com. Oct. 2001)

(5) Dharma and Karma were partners sharing profits and losses in the ratio of 3:2. The following was the balance sheet of the firm as on 31-12-2011.

Liabilities		Amount	Assets	Amount
Capital A/cs :	Dharma	75,160	Machinery	72,000
	Karma	44,080	Motor car (2)	12,000
Loans:	Dharma –	30,000	Investments	32,000
	Karma –	800	Stock	40,000
Creditors		25,000	Debtors	35,000
Bank overdraft		15,960		
		1,91,000		1,91,000

The partners desired to dissolve the firm and accept the offer of Viswaroopa Ltd., to purchase their business. The company agreed on the following terms:

(a) to take over machinery and stock and
(b) that the purchase consideration of ₹ 2,00,000 was satisfied by cash payment of ₹ 1,10,000 and the balance by allotment of 9,000 shares of ₹ 10 each.
(c) Karma took over motor car at the valuation ₹ 8,500 and Dharma the other car at ₹ 3,500.
(d) Cash realised as sale of investments amounted to ₹ 31,000. The debtors realised ₹ 30,000 and the creditors were settled for ₹ 24,000.
(e) The cost of winding up amounted to ₹ 1,500.
(f) The partners agreed to divide the share in proportion to their profit sharing ratio.

Prepare necessary ledger accounts to close the books of the firm.

Index